Anna & Anders Jeppsson

Hans-Ove Ohlsson

Outdoor Carpentry

Translation by Carol Huebscher Rhoades

Schiffer Publishing Ltd®

4880 Lower Valley Road • Atglen, PA 19310

Preface

Our ambition with *Outdoor Carpentry* was to produce a book with a wide appeal. We wanted a comprehensive book with lots of carpentry projects for outdoor life, socializing, gardening, play, and storage in the yard.

Perhaps the most important target group is, understandably, everyone interested in woodwork—or who wants to begin. Through a mix of small and large projects with varying levels of difficulty, we planned a book that would be just as suitable for beginners as for hobbyists who regularly do woodwork. If you've never done woodwork before, you should perhaps begin with some of the simpler projects and then go for some bigger challenges later. Those who are more familiar with woodworking might instead choose to build a shed, a porch, or perhaps something smaller to "relax with," such as a strawberry tower for the children.

Another important target group that we want to reach is people who have plenty of ideas but who doesn't necessarily need to make and build everything themselves. For them, we've tried to make an inspiring book with many fine photos that they, in turn, can put into the hands of a family member or someone in the circle of friends and relatives who is interested in carpentry. This can also result in several exciting new projects.

With *Outdoor Carpentry*, we hope many people will think, "I can actually build this myself!" Even if you don't find exactly what you want, you will find inspiration and help as you leaf through all the pictures and instructions for the projects. Supplement, draw from, and change the drawings to suit your needs.

We hope our choices have been made well so that, from the book's approximately forty-five different projects, you'll find one or more that you want to make yourself or that you'll find ideas to develop following your own tastes. Perhaps you'll find something that you didn't even know you wanted!

Enjoy!

Anna and Anders Jeppsson
Hans-Ove Ohlsson

Table of Contents

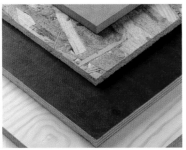

Gardening

For many people, plants and flowers are important for enjoying the yard. They provide color and beauty, and they smell good. They are also peaceful after a stressful day. You can use plants to create space in the garden. If you combine a variety of plants that flower at different times with evergreens, it is possible to enjoy plants all year round.

Perhaps you need some flowerboxes so you can grow flowers on the terrace or at the entryway, or maybe you need a trellis on which clematis and other climbing plants can cling. Or, why not build a planting table where you have everything you require for your planting chores. If you want to feel the soil between your fingers, you can build a hotbed for starting veggies and other plants.

Use pressure-treated wood if the structure will come into contact with the ground; otherwise you can use regular wood that will be finished afterwards. See more about finishing on page 118.

On the next few pages, you'll find projects for anyone who enjoys gardening.

Planting table

Durability and practicality are important qualities for a planting table. Both of these criteria are met by this attractive example that has trays made with durable plywood. A top shelf with hooks attached makes it easy for you to work there. The stand is built of rough-sawn pine painted with white exterior paint. If you set the planting table in a quiet and secluded spot in the garden, you'll create a little oasis where you can forget the time.

Materials

1 x 4 (¾ x 3½"):
    4 pieces each 46½" (A)
    4 pieces each 24" (B)
    2 pieces each 22½" (C)
    2 pieces each 36" (D)
    2 pieces each 48" (E)
    1 piece 45"(F)
    4 pieces each 30½" (G)
    2 pieces each 8" (H)

1 x 6 (¾ x 5½"):
    1 piece 48¾" (I)
    1 piece 47¼" (J)
    2 pieces each 25½" (K)

½" plywood:
    1 piece 25⅛ x 48" (L)
    1 piece 24 x 46½'" (M)

Galvanized wood screws
Glue for outdoor use
Exterior paint
Hooks

Instructions

1. Cut pieces A, B, and C for the two frames that will hold the bench shelves. Glue and screw them together.

2. Cut the front legs D and back legs E. Glue and screw them securely to the frame. Note that the frames should be attached ¾" in from the outer edge of the legs so that the diagonal boards G will fit in.

3. Cut board F, which connects the back legs at the top. Glue and screw it into place.

4. Cut the four diagonals G at a 45° angle on both ends. They should be 30½" on the long side for a good fit. Glue and screw them into place.

5. Cut the two triangles H for the braces from an 8" piece; glue and screw them securely at the top of the back legs.

6. Cut shelf I and glue and screw it firmly to the top.

7. Cut pieces J and K for the back and sides of the top bench tray. Cut a groove ½" deep and ⅜" wide beneath the sides K and the back J. Round the top front corner of sides K.

8. Paint the entire construction, including pieces K and J for the tray.

9. Cut bench shelves L and M (or order them already cut by the lumberyard). Sand and seal the cut surfaces.

10. Insert the lower shelf M (tilt it and push it in from the side).

11. Glue and screw on tray sides K and back J to shelf L. Use thinner screws and counterbore. Make sure that all the pieces fit, then glue and screw it into place. Put the shelf into place and then attach it with a few screws.

12. Screw on the hooks below the shelf.

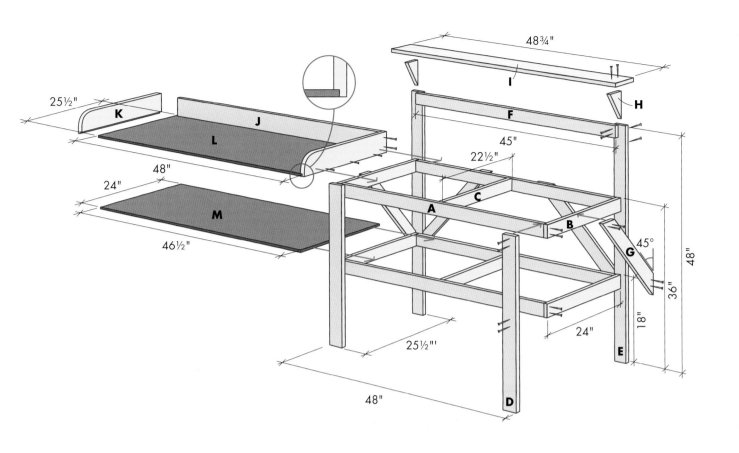

48¾"

I

H

25½"

K

J

F

45"

22½"

L

C

A

B

48"

24"

G

45°

M

48"

25½"'

24"

E

46½"

36"

18"

48"

D

*Adjust the height of
the table for the person
who will use it most.*

Flowerbox

This flowerbox is built with strips of wood painted white and rests on brackets. The space between the strips gives the box a pleasant and less compact look. Plant the flowers in inexpensive plastic flower boxes or pots, setting them down into the box where they'll be hidden effectively.

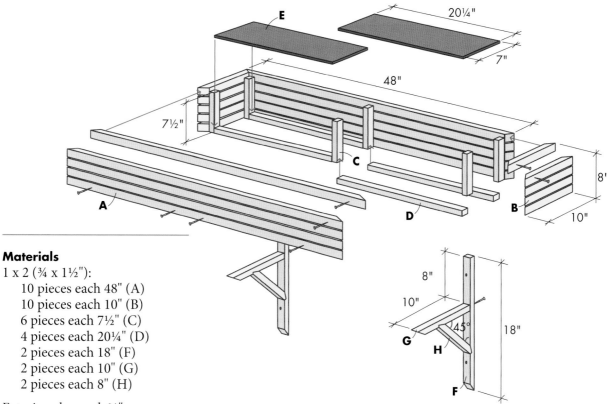

Materials

1 x 2 (¾ x 1½"):
    10 pieces each 48" (A)
    10 pieces each 10" (B)
    6 pieces each 7½" (C)
    4 pieces each 20¼" (D)
    2 pieces each 18" (F)
    2 pieces each 10" (G)
    2 pieces each 8" (H)

Exterior plywood, ½":
    2 pieces each 7" x 20¼" (E)

Glue for outdoor use
Galvanized wood screws
2 plastic flower boxes
Exterior paint

Instructions

If you want to use plastic flower boxes as "inner pots," recalculate all the measurements to fit them. Instead of using plastic boxes and the "inner pots," you can line the inside of this box with plastic. Attach the plastic with a hot glue and staples.

Box

Consider the measurements given in the Materials list as finished measurements. You might need to start with slightly longer boards for those that will be mitered on the ends.

1. Cut all the pieces for the box, A-D. It will be easiest to use a crosscut saw and miter box.

2. Leaving a ⅛" gap between them, glue and screw the slats for the long side A together with the three uprights C. The spaces between the uprights should be 20¼".

3. Glue and firmly screw in rails D, which will support the bottom shelf E.

4. Glue and screw together the long sides with the frame pieces B.

5. Paint the flowerbox in your choice of color.

6. Cut the plywood for the bottom shelves E and seal the cut surfaces. Set the pieces into the flowerbox.

Brackets

1. Cut the uprights and the horizontals F and G to the correct measurements.

2. Glue and screw them together.

3. Rough cut the diagonal supports H and lay them over the assembled parts at a 45° angle. Mark the cutting lines for the pieces. Cut and glue them together; clamp, and let dry.

4. Bore holes for attaching to the wall.

5. Paint the brackets in your choice of color.

Finishing

Set up the brackets and put the box into place. To make sure that the box is firmly in place, lift the bottom shelf and screw the box into the brackets.

13

Hotbed

A small hotbed for starting little seedlings or herbs, it serves equally well for a little garden on the balcony or as an addition to a large greenhouse. The shelves are moveable and, when the plants have grown a bit larger, you just have to move them down a "floor." Watering is easy because there are drain holes at the bottom. You can give the plants a shower right in the box!

Materials

Plywood, ¼":
    2 pieces each 36½ x 12" (A)
    2 pieces each 24 x 21" (B)
    1 piece 36 x 24" (F)
    2 pieces each 8 x 24" (H)

Rails & Stiles, 1 x 2 (¾ x 1½"):
    4 pieces each 14" rough (C)
    2 pieces each 35" (D)
    3 pieces each 21" (G)
    8 pieces each 16" (M)
    2 pieces each 36½" (N)
    2 pieces each 36½" planed to ⅜" thickness (O)

Rails, 1 x 1 (¾ x ¾"):
    2 pieces each 35" (E)

Handles & rails, 1 x 4 (¾ x 3½"):
    4 pieces each 5" (I)
    1 piece 36½" (K)
    1 piece 37½" (L)

Rods, ¾" diameter:
    2 pieces each 16" (J)

Plexiglas (or glass):
    6 pieces each 10⅝ x 14¾"(P)

Hinges: 6
Glue for exterior use
Galvanized wood screws
Exterior paint

Instructions

1. Begin by cutting the long sides A and the gables B from the plywood. The tip of the gable should be trimmed to leave a ¾-inch flat surface. The top edge of the long sides should be beveled at the same angle as the gable so that they will align when they are assembled.

2. Cut rails C, D, and E, which will be placed on the inside of the long sides. Glue and firmly screw in the corner pieces C, the legs, ¼" from the edge. Note that they should extend down, below the bottom of the sides, approximately ⅜". This will provide ventilation.

3. Glue and firmly screw the horizontal rails D and E in place. E should be about 6" from the bottom.

4. Glue and screw in the two rails G in the lower edge on the gables B. Glue and firmly screw the gables B to uprights C.

5. Glue and screw the third rail G across the bottom at the centers of rails D.

5. Cut the bottom board F with notches for the corner pieces. Glue and screw them firmly to the bottom rails G and D.

7. Bore a few drain holes in the bottom board F.

8. Cut a couple of shelves H, which will lie loosely on the top rails E of the long sides.

9. Cut 4 blocks I for the handles. They should be 5" long. Cut off the corners and bore holes for the rods J.

10. Insert rods J. Glue and securely screw the handles to gables B from the inside.

11. Cut board K, which will connect the points of the gables. Make a ¾ x ¾" notch for the gables in each end. Glue and screw K firmly in place.

12. Cut the covering batten L which lies on top of the frame. Bevel off the top surface on both sides of the center with a plane. Glue and screw it firmly to board K.

13. Rails and stiles M and N for the lid should be rabbeted with a router. The outer rails M should be rabbeted on the inside edge. The lower rails O are planed down to ⅜". The top edge of rail N should be beveled at the same angle as the gables, so, when the lid closes, it lies correctly. Join the stiles and rails with a lap joint. Glue them together, set in a press, and let dry.

14. Assemble the lid with three hinges on each side.

15. Paint the entire construction with exterior paint.

16. Attach the Plexiglas with latex sealant. Lay a narrow bead in the groove, press the glass into place, and seal along the glass. Prop the lids up so that they rest horizontally until the sealant has completely hardened.

The handles make it easy to move the hotbed and Plexiglas keeps the weight down.

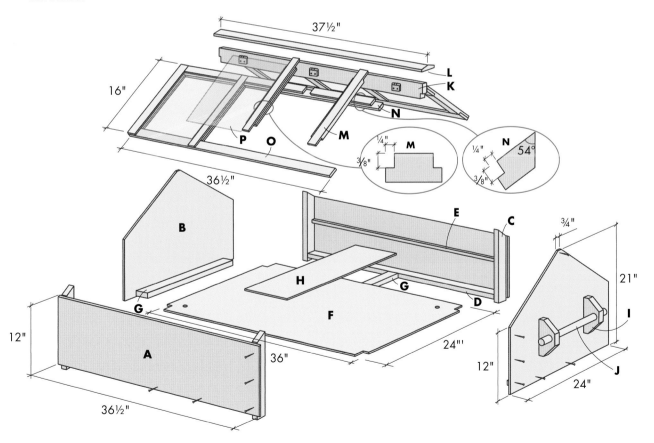

17

Wall trellis

Clematis grows best when it can climb a bit out from the wall. This photo shows a simple and attractive structure that gives the plants a chance to "breathe." The trellis is constructed with pressure-treated wood, and the reinforcing bars are attached to the wall with flat hanger screws.

Materials

Pressure-treated wood boards, 2 x 2 (1½ x 1½"):
    4 pieces each 12" (A)

Reinforcing bars (rebar), ¼" diameter':
    3 pieces each 72" (B)

Flat hanger screws, 6": 4
Wood screws: 4

Instructions

1. Cut the four bars A.

2. Bore 3 holes in each bar. The holes should be large enough that the reinforcing rods B can be inserted, while fitting a bit tightly.

3. Insert all three reinforcing rods in one of the bars.

4. Insert rods into one bar after the other, hammering them into place with a wood mallet.

5. Measure the placement of the flat hanger (flat eye lag) screws (for example, two at the top and two on the next-to-bottom board) and screw them into the wall.

6. Set up the trellis so that it rests on the flat hanger screws and then attach with screws.

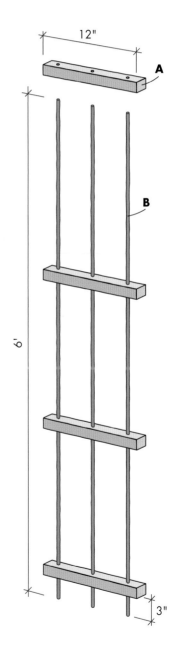

Flat hanger screws are most often used by pipelayers to attach pipes to a roof.

Double flowerbox

The goal was to have flowers on both sides of the fence.
The result was a double flowerbox, overflowing with summer
flowers, to hang over the railing. The box resembles an English
hanging basket, but it is larger. The shelf built into the center
provides a place for some small terracotta pots.

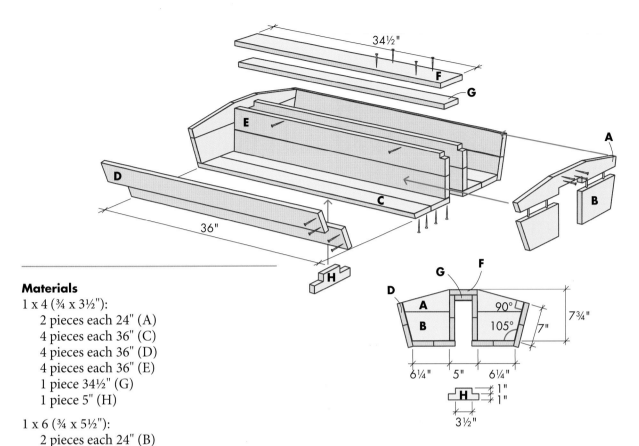

Materials

1 x 4 (¾ x 3½"):
    2 pieces each 24" (A)
    4 pieces each 36" (C)
    4 pieces each 36" (D)
    4 pieces each 36" (E)
    1 piece 34½" (G)
    1 piece 5" (H)

1 x 6 (¾ x 5½"):
    2 pieces each 24" (B)
    1 piece 34½" (F)

Wood screws
Glue for exterior use
Exterior paint

Instructions

This flowerbox was built to fit a railing with a cap piece that is 2¾" wide. If your fence cap has a different width, adjust the box measurements accordingly.

1. Cut pieces A and B for the gables a bit larger than the final measurements (about 2 feet long).

2. Glue the pieces together with wood glue, clamp, and let the glue dry.

3. Draw and cut the gables. The notch should be 7" deep and 4¾" wide.

4. Cut the base boards C. Note that the two outer boards are also cut at an angle on one long side. Glue and screw the boards firmly together beneath the gables.

5. Cut all the side and center boards D and E. Cut a notch ¾ x ¾" on the ends of the two top center boards. Glue and screw the boards in place.

6. Cut the two boards F and G, which will form the shelf. The lower board (G) fits firmly between boards E. Glue and screw them together and then glue and screw the lid into place.

7. Cut one small block H that will be pushed through the fence and between the boxes. (The block must be set into place before the boxes are filled with soil.)

8. Paint the flowerbox.

9. Set the box in place and lock it into place with the block.

You can plant directly into the box or line the inside with plastic first.

21

Plant spire

A decorative and practical structure for roses and other climbing plants. This spire featured a finial top turned on a lathe, but you are only limited by your imagination in this regard. If you don't want to fashion your own top, you can buy large knobs at the gardening center.

Materials

Cut wood, ¾ x ¾"
   (these can be ripped from 1x stock)

Galvanized wood screws
Spire top/knob
Exterior stain

Instructions

1. Cut the pieces for the four legs A so that they are each 60" long. If you want to make the spire more stable, cut two of the legs longer so you can stick them into the ground a bit. This is particularly recommended if the spire will be in a windy spot.

2. Lay two sets of two legs on the ground with one end together and the other spaced 18" apart (at ground level).

3. Roughly cut the crossbars B by measuring where they will sit, mark with a lead pencil, and cut. Counterbore and screw them into place. Trim to fit legs.

4. Measure and cut the diagonal rails C. Counterbore and screw them into place.

5. Lay the assembled sets of legs on the ground with the tips together at the top end and with 18" between the legs at the other end (at ground level). Attach the crossbars and diagonal rails as before.

6. Turn the spire in the opposite direction and assemble as for the first side.

7. The finial was turned on a lathe but, if you don't have access to a lathe, you can look for something else to place on top or leave the spire without any top decoration.

8. Finish the spire with a coating of stain.

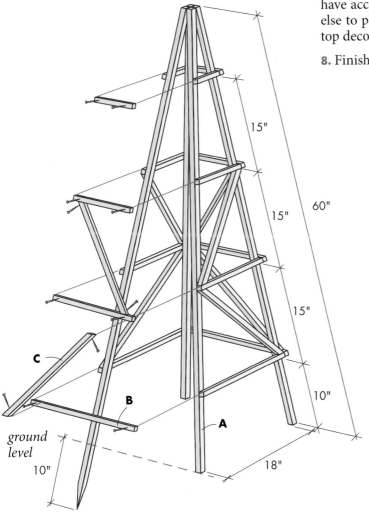

Strawberry tower

Wild strawberries are part of childhood summers. They are easy to grow, and it feels so luxurious to pick them and pop them right into your mouth. The strawberry tower is simple to construct. It doesn't even need a perfect finish, so why not let the children join in and do some woodwork? Then they can plant the strawberries themselves and take care of their plants. Imagine—your very own wild strawberry patch!

Materials

1 x 6 (¾ x 5½")
- 2 pieces each 22½'" (A)
- 2 pieces each 24" (B)
- 2 pieces each 13½" (C)
- 2 pieces each 15" (D)
- 2 pieces each 4½" (E)
- 2 pieces each 6" (F)
- 4 pieces each 5½" (G)

Cut wood, ¾ x ¾" (can be ripped from 1x)
- 4 pieces each 10" (H)
- 4 pieces each 13½" (I)

½" exterior plywood:
- 1 piece 22½ x 22½" (J)

Wood screws
Glue for exterior use
Exterior paint

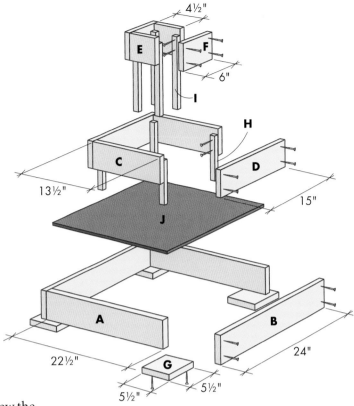

Instructions

1. Cut pieces A–F for the frame and legs G.

2. Begin with the bottom frame. Glue and screw the four sides A and B together. Glue and screw the short legs G firmly to the underside.

3. Make the center frame. Begin by gluing and screwing legs H firmly to the short sides C. The legs should extend 4½" down from the boards. Firmly screw and glue in the two longer sides D.

4. Construct the top frame with pieces E and F the same way but now the legs should extend down 9".

5. Paint the frame and the legs.

6. Cut shelf J from the form plywood and seal the cut surfaces.

7. Place shelf J in the lower frame. Set the rest of the frames into place; fill with soil and plants.

The durability of the planter is limited when the soil, as here, is in direct contact with the wood. However, the strawberry tower should last for many years, and then you'll have the pleasure of building a new one.

When the season changes, the strawberry tower might become an herb tower.

Freestanding trellis

Climbing plants thrive best when they can grow with a lot of air circulating around them. This freestanding trellis simply and pleasantly divides the garden into different spaces. It fits just as easily into a small yard as a very large one. Depending on which plants you choose to grow, the trellis can protect your privacy either minimally or very effectively.

Materials

For one section:

Posts, 4 x 4 (3½ x 3½")
  2 pieces each 72" (A); 84" for doorway pieces

1 x 2 (¾ x 1½")
  9 pieces each 57" (B)
  8 pieces each 72" (C)

For one doorway with the same width as one section:
1 x 4 (¾ x 3½")
  2 pieces each 96" (D)

Lumber, 2 x 2 (1¾ x 1¾")
  11 pieces each 15" (E)

Plinths: 2
Hexagonal bolts, nuts, and washers for the plinths
Wood screws
Exterior paint

Instructions for the trellis

1. Bury the plinths (see page 105).

2. Cut posts A. Cut them at an angle at the top so water will run off.

3. Sink the posts and screw them firmly to the plinths.

4. Screw in the two vertical rails B that adjoin posts A. If the sections are angled with respect to each other, the rails should be cut to the actual angle (see the details within the red circles on the illustration).

5. Screw in the horizontal rails C, cutting at an angle on the end where the sections are turned towards each other.

6. Finally, screw on the rest of the vertical rails B.

Instructions for the doorway

7. Screw the horizontal boards D together.

8. Set into place, center, and screw in the two outer rails E.

9. Space the remaining rails E evenly apart and screw in.

10. Finish the trellis and doorway with top coat paint.

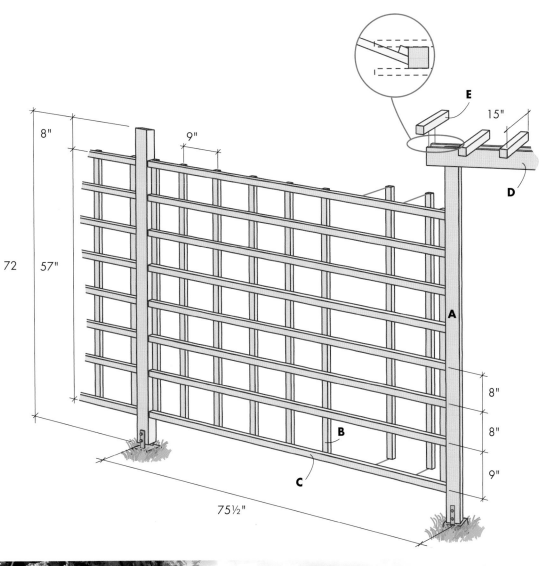

8"

9"

72

57"

E

15"

A

8"

8"

B

9"

D

C

75½"

Terraces, wood decks and terrace roof

All single-family homes can have an outdoor area that functions as a natural extension of the house during the summer months. It's the place where we gather and socialize, eat and play. We have parties there or tend the grill for a cozy supper with the entire family on a weekday evening.

A wood terrace or a wood deck provides a soft and pleasant surface to walk on. With the right foundation, it will last for generations and look even nicer as it ages. If you also plan a roof, you'll be protected in case of unexpected bad weather.

Planning

All outdoor constructions should fit with the house and its surroundings. That also applies to a terrace or a wood deck. Begin by taking out some paper and a pencil. Draw your lot and the house's placement on the lot. Take the compass directions into consideration. Is there a difference of level between the surface of the lot and the house? You can solve that by laying a wood deck at ground level with stairs up to the house or by constructing a terrace level with the house and stairs down to ground level. Do you want a permanent roof over the terrace or would it be better with a marquee or a sail? Draw! Think!

Don't forget to talk with your neighbors so they are familiar with your plans, even if they don't have to approve them. It always helps to be good neighbors.

Additional considerations

• An outdoor area also functions as an extra room during the summer. Consider the entrance from the house.

• If you have some options in choosing the placement for the outdoor area, you have to decide if you want to have morning or afternoon sun. Of course you can build a smaller patio in order to be able, for example, to eat breakfast in the morning sunshine, and a larger one in another place for coffee breaks, suppers, and parties with family and friends, if that works.

• Do you need to complete the outdoor area with wind or privacy protection? And why not build a roof over the space? It will save you on many rainy days.

• Build your terrace so that it is child-safe and won't cause accidents.

• Don't make the terrace too small. After all, you'll be spending most of the time on the terrace when you are out in the yard.

• From the very beginning, plan so that you can build out your terrace or add a roof overhead at a later date.

• You can often build a terrace or a wood deck without a building permit, but there are exceptions. If you want a roof over the outdoor structure there are rules for what you can and cannot do. Read more about "Rules and Regulations" on page 114.

• There are several different types of materials to choose from for a terrace or wood deck. Read more about "Common types of wood and their characteristics" on page 107. For the framework, UC4B-treated wood should be used because it either comes in contact with the ground or is difficult to change out.

Basic instructions

• A terrace needs some type of foundation on plinths when the level of the house is higher than the surface of the ground, or if the ground slopes. Even a terrace roof needs a stable foundation. Read more about foundations on page 105.

• A simple way to construct a wood deck is to build it directly on the ground, where the boards lie on the concrete blocks. See an example on page 36.

We hope you'll be inspired by the projects on the following pages.

Large terrace

A terrace at ground level can advantageously divide a large, flat grass surface. You can reach this terrace directly from the living room of a single-story house, so it functions like a large, extra room. You can set the table here for many guests on mild, summer evenings and still have room to spare. And, when the mood strikes, why not dance to the music heard through the open terrace door?

Terrace

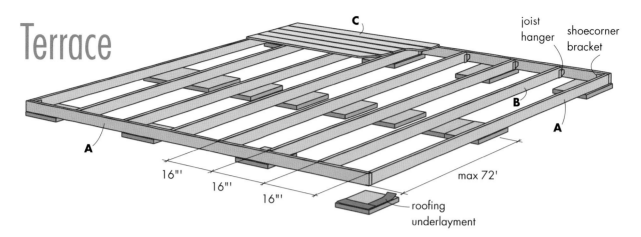

joist hanger

shoecorner bracket

C

B

A

A

16"'

16"'

16"'

max 72'

roofing underlayment

Materials
Fiber cloth
Shingle
Sand or gravel
Garden paving stones
Roofing underlayment
Pressure-treated wood, 2 x 6 (1½ x 5½") (A and B)
Pressure-treated decking wood, 5/4 x 6 (1 x 5½")(C)
Decking screws
Anchor screws
Joist hangers
Angle brackets

Instructions

1. Remove the soil to a depth of about 6" over the entire surface. The depth depends on how close the terrace will be to the surface of the lawn.

2. Lay out the fiber cloth, fill it with about 2" of gravel and compress. Add a layer of sand or gravel about one inch thick.

3. Lay out the garden paving stones as supports for the wood deck, following the illustration. Use a level or laser instrument to ensure that all the paving stones are set at the same level.

4. Cut the pieces for the deck frame A, lay them on the concrete plates with roofing underlayment between the stones and the wood, and then screw them together with the angle brackets. Make sure that the frame is completely straight.

5. Attach the joist hangers on the frame 16" on center (c/c). Use the anchor screws. Set in boards B and attach them to the joist hangers with anchor screws. Lay roofing underlayment between the concrete and wood.

6. Use the level to ensure that all the pieces are completely level and straight. Wedge up if necessary.

7. If the wood is too low and there is the possibility that the frame will be in contact with the ground, wrap the wood with roofing underlayment and surround it with gravel.

8. Screw in the decking boards C, letting the ends extend over the edge, and then cut all the pieces at the same time.

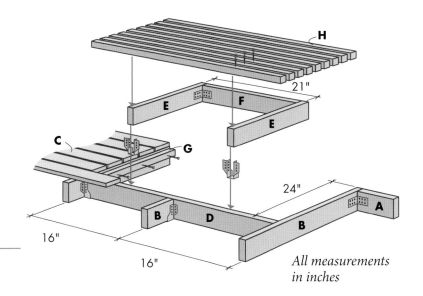

21"

24"

16"

16"

All measurements in inches

Light well

Materials

Pressure-treated wood, 2 x 6 (1½ x 5½")
    A and B = included with the materials
    for the terrace
    1 piece 30½" (D)

Pressure-treated wood, 2 x 6 (1½ x 5½")
    2 pieces each 2' (E)
    1 piece 21" (F)

Pressure-treated wood, 2 x 2 (1½ x 1½")
    2 pieces each 24" (G)
    9 pieces each 30½" (H)

Decking screws
Anchor screws
Joist hangers
Corner brackets

Instructions

1. Assemble the terrace frame A and boards B so that a sufficient opening for the light well can be built in front of the cellar window. Attach the lintel D to boards B.

2. Cut the decking C even with boards B.

3. Screw the two support boards G securely 1" down on the short sides of the opening.

4. Screw the joist hangers securely to board D in front of boards E at 21" on center.

5. Join boards E and F with the corner brackets.

6. Space the rails H about ¾" apart and screw them firmly to boards E.

7. Lay the lid on loosely.

Pool deck

Your own pool! Is there anything more inviting? The feeling of vacation while lying on rubber floats and bobbing around in the waves on the turquoise-colored water the whole summer. But you don't need to be a water lover to enjoy the pool environment. It can be just as nice to sit on the edge with your feet in the water and philosophize. And, if the desire strikes, the deck is big enough for all your friends and acquaintances who long for a real pool party.

The pool's construction and size, as well as the layout of the yard and differences in ground level, determine how the pool deck is constructed. Here, we show the principles for how to build a pool deck if the pool has a steel shell with a liner and the ground is somewhat uneven. These principles can also be applied to other pools and lot conditions. The calculations are worked out for this particular situation.

Materials

All wood is pressure-treated.

Dimensional lumber:
    A = 2 x 4 (1½ x 3½")
    B = 2 x 8 (1½ x 7½")
    C = 2 x 3 (1½ x 2½")
    F = 2 x 8 (1½ x 7½")
    G1 and G2 = 2 x 6 (1½ x 5½")

Decking wood, 5/4 x 6 (1 x 5½") (H)

Concrete tiles (D)
Plinths (E)
Hexagonal bolts, washers, and nuts for the plinths
Roofing underlayment
French wood screws with washers
Angle brackets
Anchor screws
Wood screws

Instructions

1. Lay the pool cloth (liner) around boards A and screw it securely from underneath, through the steel shell, using French wood screws and washers.

2. Screw the rails C into the edge board B with wood screws, and don't forget to counterbore. Trim the joined boards to the correct lengths.

3. Lay board B over A and screw it securely from underneath, through A, but not through the steel edge. Use French wood screws with washers.

4. Place the concrete tiles D at the right level. Make sure all are level.

5. Place out the plinths E (see page 105) and assemble the support beams F so that their top edge is at the same level as the plates D. Lay a plank over D and F and make sure they are level.

6. Lay out the floor joists G1 and G2 and assemble them with the angle brackets and anchor screws. Lay the roofing underlayment between the boards and the concrete tiles.

7. Screw in the decking boards H.

8. If the pool has curved lines, for example, by a stairwell, boards A, B, and C should be cut into short pieces that fit the curved line and then joined the same way as the straight edges.

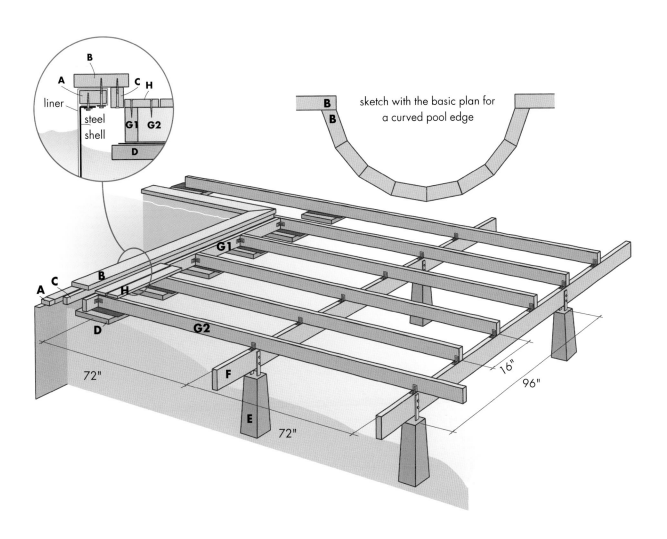

B

A   C H

liner

steel
shell

G1 G2

D

sketch with the basic plan for
a curved pool edge

B
B

G1

B

A C

H

D

G2

F

E

72"

16"

96"

72"

*The wood privacy fence frames the
pool area and also keeps curious
neighborhood children from coming
too close. The lamps around the fence
emit a soft light as evening falls.*

Deck around a large tree

When building a terrace, incorporating an existing tree is a lovely way to create a quiet oasis—a place for relaxing, having a coffee break, dinner or "a dance on the pier." The tree doesn't need to be very big to create a good effect. The size of the terrace is fitted to the lot and, of course, what you want to use it for. If you are lucky enough to have a big, 100-year-old oak growing on your lot, a tree that provides shade on hot summer days, the terrace will be favorite place number one.

Materials

Pressure-treated wood, 2 x 6 (1½ x 5½")
    4 pieces each 12' (A)
    2 pieces each 13' (B)
    2 pieces each 12' (F)
    20 pieces each 6" (E)

Pressure-treated wood, 2 x 6 (1½ x 5½")
    16 pieces each 46½" (C)
    2 pieces each approx. 2' (D), measurements
    determined by diameter of the tree.

Decking wood, 5/4 x 6 (1 x 5½") (G)

Molded plinths with post fasteners (see page 106): 12
Hexagonal bolts, washers, and nuts for the plinths
Concrete tiles: 4
Roofing underlayment
Joist hangers: 36
Angle brackets: 16
Anchor screws
Wood screws

Instructions

1. Set out the plinths (see page 106).

2. Smooth out the ground surface where the concrete plates will lie. Spread out a layer of gravel and pack it down hard. Lay out the concrete plates.

3. Set boards A into the post fasteners on the plinths. Check with a level, bore, and screw in securely. Note that the wood shouldn't rest against the concrete; wedge under it until they are screwed firmly together.

4. Lay strips of roofing underlayment on the concrete plates and wedge under the boards A until they are level.

5. Join the covering boards B to the boards A with the angle brackets.

6. Join boards C with boards A using joist hangers. The boards nearest the tree trunk are placed approx. 2" from this. Join boards D the same way.

7. Screw in the spacer blocks E firmly and then the covering boards F. Screw the covering boards B and F together. Trim the ends of B so they are flush with F.

8. Screw the decking boards G firmly to the frame spacing them approx. ⅛" apart. Shape around the tree.

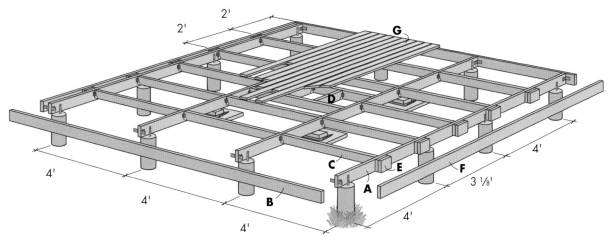

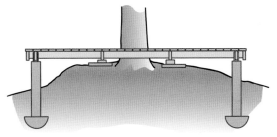

The tree stands on a small hill. For that reason, a foundation combining plinths and concrete tiles on the ground was necessary. It is also inadvisable to dig holes for the plinths too close to the tree. If the yard is flat, you won't need any plinths.

Terrace roof

The roof serves as a protection against both sun and rain. The reinforced glass filters the sun's rays and makes a pretty light, and, when it is raining, it is much quieter than a plastic roof. The skeleton is built as a frame in a comfortable work place on the grounds, taken apart, and then reassembled later, piece by piece *in situ*.

Materials

2 x 6" (1½ x 5½"):
    1 piece 120" (A)
    6 pieces each 80" (D)

4 x 4 (3½ x 3½")
    2 pieces each 96" (B)

2 x 8 (1½ x 7½")
    1 piece 120" (C)

2 x 2 (1½ x 1½")
    2 pieces, each 120" (E)

Tempered glass, or as shown here, wired glass:
    5 pieces, each 24" x 80" (F),
    ordered from a glass store

Aluminum channels, including sealing strips:
    6 pieces (G), ordered from a glass store

Plinths: 2
Hexagonal bolts with washers
    and nuts for the plinths
Nail plugs or another type of fastening for
    the wall, depending on wall composition
Wood screws
Gutter and drainpipe with fittings

Instructions

1. Cut all the pieces with the notches for the roof frame. Lay out the roof on a flat surface and check to make sure everything fits. Make the notches deep enough so that all the parts will lie at the same level along the top.

The roof slopes at 4°, but the support joists A and C do not slope. The notches in the roof beams D for A and C should therefore be cut at a 4° angle. The support battens E follow the slope of the roof.

Cut the notches by laying all the pieces that are alike together, holding them together with clamps. Measure and draw the lines carefully and make several cuts with a circular saw. Remove the clamps and clean the cut with a chisel.

2. Disassemble the structure and finish all the pieces.

3. Attach the support joist A to the wall with nail plugs, expansion bolts, or whatever is suitable for the house façade.

4. Set out the plinths for posts B (see page 105). In this case, the plinths stand with their center points 70" from the wall of the house, where the support joist is attached.

5. Screw the posts B firmly into the post fasteners on the plinths. Make sure they are vertical.

6. Screw joist C into the posts B. To make sure that the slope of the roof is correct, the top edge of joist C (in this case) is 5" lower than the top edge of joist A.

7. Set the roof beams D into place and screw them in firmly.

8. Set the support battens E into place and screw them in firmly.

9. Lay the glass in place and attach it with the aluminum channels and screws.

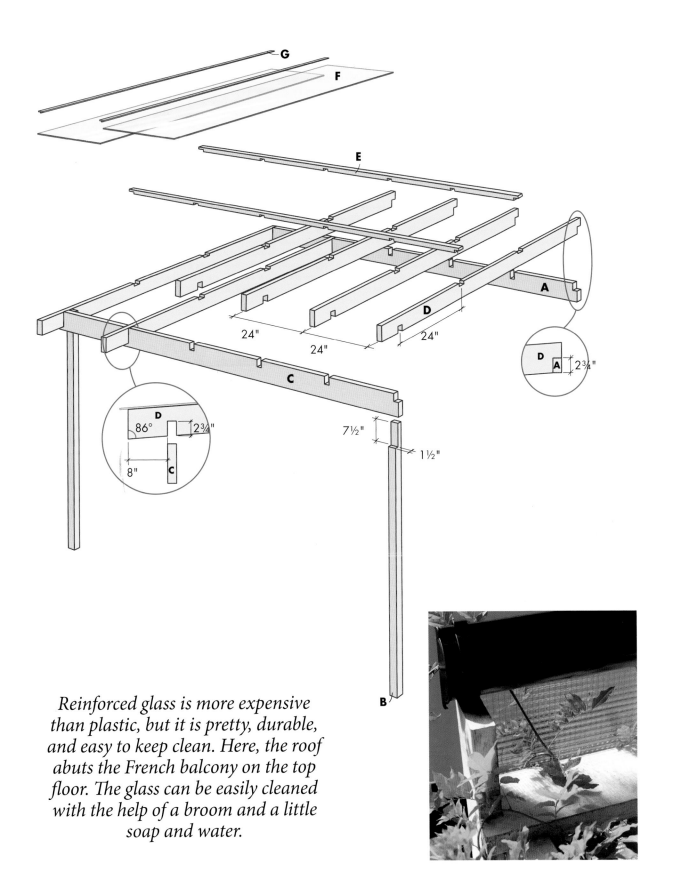

G

F

E

A

D

24"

24"

24"

D

A

2¾"

C

D

86°

2¾"

8"

C

7½"

1½"

B

Reinforced glass is more expensive than plastic, but it is pretty, durable, and easy to keep clean. Here, the roof abuts the French balcony on the top floor. The glass can be easily cleaned with the help of a broom and a little soap and water.

Picket fences, gates, privacy fences, and doorways

A fence marks the boundaries of a lot and creates "territory;" a privacy fence additionally creates seclusion and privacy. Traditionally, we build low fences, but smaller lots and closer buildings have created the need for higher and more solid fences to establish a sense of space and seclusion in the yard. Because a picket or privacy fence around a yard is often the first thing visitors and passersby see when getting near or going by your house, you should try to style the fence shape to suit the house and its surroundings.

A gate can give a welcoming impression and should blend well into the fence and the surroundings. At the same time, the gate has the function of demarcating, keeping the outside out or the inside in. A gate should be resistant to stress and wear, so should be sized well, preferably with an especially good frame.

The doorway often has a practical function, as well as an aesthetic one. Simply put, you just have to be able to open the fence to bring in some type of vehicle.

Planning

Begin by studying your house and its surroundings. Take out a pencil and paper and sketch some options for the fence. Consider how you use the yard, where the patio is, which direction the wind usually blows from, the inward and outward views, etc. Talk with your neighbors. It is important that they feel comfortable with your fence. Perhaps you can build something together on the common property lines.

A gate is a part of a picket fence and a doorway part of a privacy fence. The design of these openings should, therefore, follow that of the fence. Consider what you want to be able to bring in through the opening. If, for example, you want to drive a truck through, the opening should be about 10' wide while an opening for pedestrian traffic doesn't need to be more than about 3' wide.

Additional considerations:

• To demarcate the property lines clearly, a fence about 24 to 30 inches high will be sufficient.

• If you want privacy for an outdoor seating area, the fence should be 48 inches high.

• If you want complete privacy, you'll need to build a solid wood fence 6 feet high; this also means that the sunlight will be deflected towards evening.

• A lattice fence offers much better wind protection than a solid fence. Turbulence builds up and then is pulled behind a solid fence (see fig. 1).

• Vertical boards make the fences seem taller, while horizontal boards make the fence look longer. Take into consideration that horizontal boards invite climbing and can therefore be dangerous to have around a pool or at the edge of a bluff.

• Oversize the entire gate or doorway. This allows for protection against undue stress from bad weather and wind as well as playing children, etc.

• Gate posts should be made with pressure-treated wood grade UC4B and the rest of the gate with grade UC3B.

• All of the hinges, screws, and other fittings should, at a minimum, be galvanized and rustproof.

• For stability, choose hinges with a length at least 2/3 the width of the gate.

• Gates and entryways should be reinforced with boards placed from the lower hinge and diagonally upwards. The diagonals should be firmly affixed and not hang down. (See fig. 2 and the individual instructions for constructing gates.)

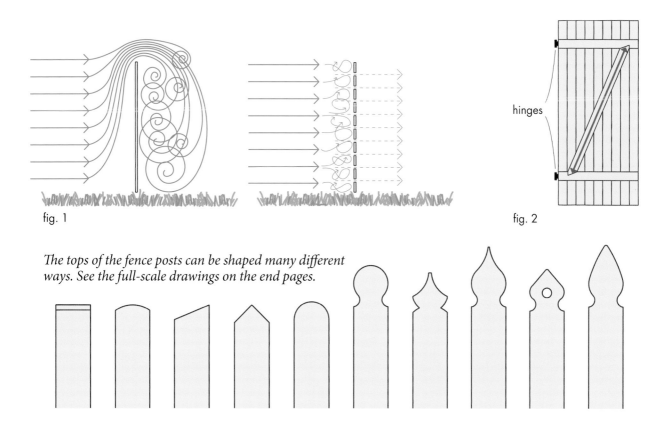

fig. 1

hinges

fig. 2

The tops of the fence posts can be shaped many different ways. See the full-scale drawings on the end pages.

51

• Think about how you want to lock the gate or doorway. Do you want to prevent someone from coming in or your small children from going out on an adventure?

• There are rules and regulations that determine where and how you can build, and very often you'll need a building permit. Read more about this on page 104.

General instructions

• All types of fences must have a suitable foundation on which to stand. Gate and doorway posts should have a stable foundation, preferably one that is even more stable than that for the fence posts. Read more about foundations on page 105.

• Consider placing the plinth post fasteners as shown in fig. 3, particularly when you build a solid wood fence.

• It is a good idea to make the gate posts a bit higher and perhaps a little thicker. That strengthens the impression of a gate and also gives it more structural integrity. (See fig. 4.)

• Be careful from the very beginning. A fence that doesn't run in a straight line isn't attractive. Begin by placing the end posts and checking with a level to make sure they are vertical. Stretch a cord between these and align the rest of the posts to it (see fig. 5). A sufficient distance between the posts is usually 6 feet, but sometimes people prefer something completely different.

• Attach the horizontal boards with construction brackets following fig. 6a or make notches in the post as shown on fig. 6b. The method with the notches is best for a picket fence, while the brackets work well for both picket and solid fences. Normally you'll use two horizontal boards for a picket fence and three for a solid fence. Do not make the notches too deep—at least 1½" of the post should remain.

Joining the horizontal boards is done at the posts. If you want to cover the joint, you can place a covering board over it (see fig. 7). In that case, you need to make a notch that corresponds exactly to the thickness of the horizontal board. If the board is 1½" thick, the post must be at least 3" thick so that there will be 1½" left in the post.

If you build the post with three parts, as shown in fig. 8, you'll have a strong post that won't crack. For a picket fence, use a 2 x 3 (1½ x 2½") for the post and two 1 x 4s (¾ x 3½") for the covering boards. The horizontal boards are 2 x 4s and are attached with brackets to the post. This type of post needs nearly exact placement of the foundation plinths, because there is not a lot of room for play when the posts are attached to the plinths. For a privacy fence, thicker dimensions must be used depending on the height and distance between the posts.

• It is a good idea to cover posts with a post cap (see fig. 9). That prevents moisture from coming into contact with the ends of the wood. The caps can be made of metal or wood, or perhaps you can cast them with concrete. If you don't want to cap the posts, then you should cut the post tops at an angle (see fig. 10). You should do the same with the horizontal boards.

• Be extra careful when you measure and construct the gate or door. Everything must be at right angles because the gate or door is a moveable part and, at the same time, must be stable.

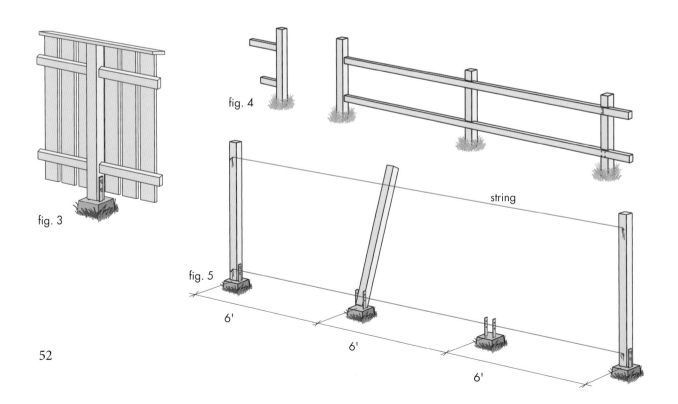

fig. 3

fig. 4

fig. 5

string

6'

6'

6'

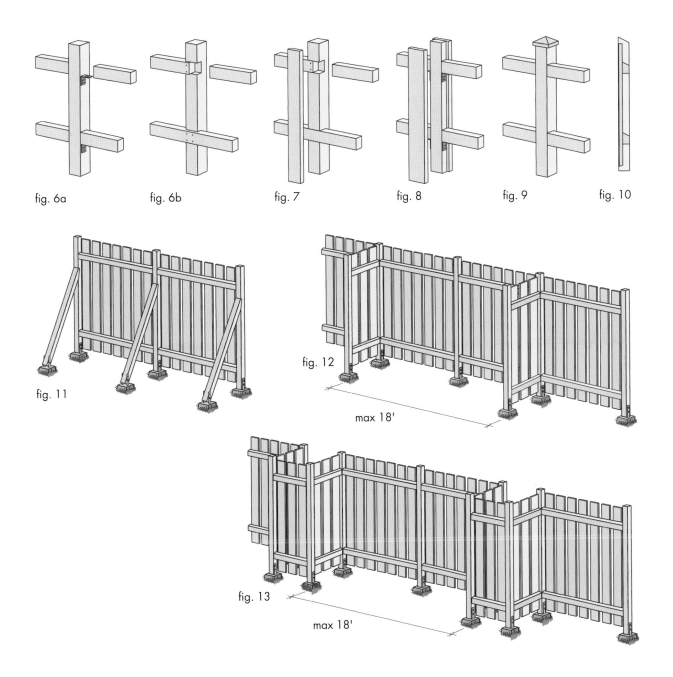

fig. 6a   fig. 6b   fig. 7   fig. 8   fig. 9   fig. 10

fig. 11

fig. 12   max 18'

fig. 13   max 18'

• The forces of the wind can greatly affect a solid wood fence, particularly if the fence is long and in a place that is very windy. It goes without saying that a good foundation is a prerequisite, but other measures must be taken into account so that the fence will remain straight well into the future. Figs. 11, 12, and 13 show some examples of methods for preventing your new fence from becoming a leaning fence.

Look through the following pages and get inspired! You'll find another solid fence on page 140.

Fence & gate

The fence follows the ground's slope, giving it a soft look. The simple contrast between the red fence stakes and the white gate works well in the countryside with the white house from the turn of the century.

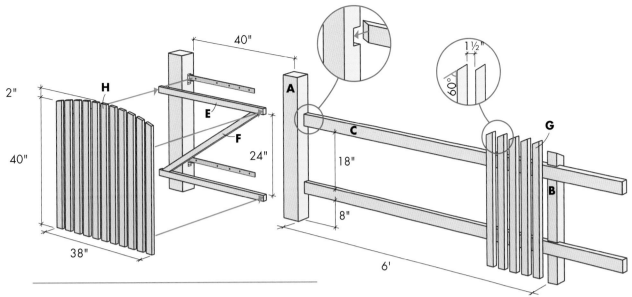

Materials
For one section of the fence and the gate.

6 x 6 (5½ x 5½")
   2 pieces each 48" (A)

4 x 4 (3½ x 3½")
   2 pieces each 36"(B) not including
   the section nearest the gate post

2 x 4 (1½ x 3½")
   2 pieces each 75½" per section (C)

2 x 3 (1½ x 2½")
   approx. 23 pieces, each 36" (G) per section
   2 pieces each 38" (E)
   1 piece 46" (F)
   11 pieces, slightly more than 42" (H)

Plinths
Hexagonal bolts, washers, and nuts for the plinths
Gate hinges: 2
Gate latch
Wood screws

Instructions for the fence
Don't forget to paint all of the parts before assembling.

1. Bury the plinths (see page 105).

2. Attach the gate posts A to the plinth post fasteners (see page 116). Make sure that the posts are vertical.

3. Make the notches in the fence posts B for horizontals C. Cut 1½"-deep grooves and chisel out.

4. Attach the fence posts B to the plinth post fasteners. Make sure that the posts are vertical.

5. Cut the joints in A for horizontals C. Cut and shape following the drawing.

6. Screw in horizontals C, joining at the center of the joint in post B.

7. Cut the pickets G with a 60° angle at the top and a small angle at the bottom for water runoff.

8. Stretch a cord at the lower ends of the pickets as they will be placed to make it easier to align them. It is also a good idea to cut a board 1½" wide as a template to ensure that all the boards are spaced equidistantly. Screw the pickets in securely, using a level to make sure that they are all vertical.

Instructions for the gate
1. Cut horizontal bars E the correct length and screw boards H to them. Begin with the two outermost boards, check for square, and then place the center boards. Arrange the remaining boards, making sure that they are spaced equally apart.

2. Cut the crossbar F after measuring the diagonal to make sure it fits correctly and then screw in to horizontals E and boards H.

3. Draw the arch for the top of the gate and cut the boards H with a jigsaw, following the line. The radius is large, so you might want to draw a template of the curve on a masonite sheet or similar flexible material and cut it out. Hammer a nail into each of the outermost slats and in the center slat just above, at the height you wish them to be. Lay the template on the gate boards, hold it against the nails, and have someone draw the curve for you.

4. Assemble the gate hinges. Begin by attaching the parts that will sit on the post. Support the gate in the correct position, make sure that everything is squared, and mark the placement of the screws. Securely screw the hinges to the gate and hang it. Finish by attaching the gate latch.

Classic gate

This pretty little gate is quite easy to construct. The cross on the bottom and the wood dowels for the "grating" make the gate well proportioned. The fence with the pointed pickets complements it nicely. As an extra little detail, we decided to trim some of the pickets to make room for a mailbox.

Materials

4 x 4 (3½ x 3½")
   2 pieces each 40"
   for the gate posts (A)
   1 for every 6' of the fence

2 x 4 (1½ x 3½")
   2 pieces each 32" (B)
   2 pieces each 38" (C)

2 x 3 (1½ x 2½")
   1 piece 32" (D)
   2 pieces each 36" (E)

Wood dowels, ¾" diameter
   8 pieces each 11" (F)

2 x 4 (1½ x 3½")
   2 pieces each 6' (G) per fence section

1 x 3 (¾ x 2½")
   Lengths each 36" (H)

Post cap (J): purchase ready-made or cut 5"square
   pieces from a 2 x 6 and route
   or bevel the upper edge

Plinths
Hexagonal bolts, washers, and nuts for the plinths
Wood dowel pins
Gate hinges: 2
Gate latch
Wood screws
Glue for exterior use
Corner brackets for the fence

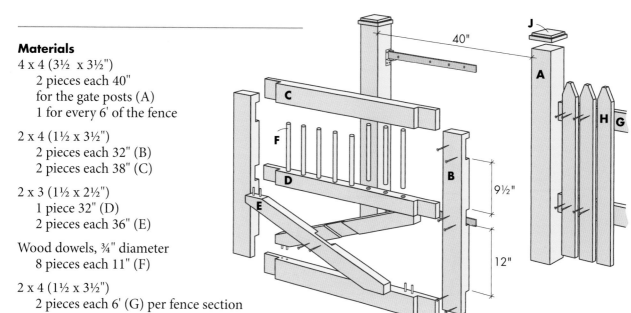

Instructions for the gate

1. Bury the plinths (see page 105).

2. Attach the gate posts A to the plinth post fasteners (see page 116). Make sure that the posts are vertical.

3. Cut B, C, and D. Join them with lap joints by making several cuts at half the thickness and then remove the wood with a chisel. File the bottom flat.

4. Lay the pieces together, holding them together with clamps. Make sure the corners are squared. Place the crossbars E exactly where they should be and mark the cutting lines and where the lap joint at the center should be.

5. Finish the E pieces and hammer in a nail where the wood dowel pins will be and then nip off the nail head.
   Lay the pieces for E together and press them against the center board D and the lower board C so that the nail marks where the pins will be.

6. Draw out the nails and bore holes for the dowel pins.

7. Bore ¾" deep holes for the rods F in the top horizontal C and the center horizontal D.

8. Assemble the pieces C and D and the rods F. Let C and D rest in parts B so that the spacing is correct. Continue the same way with parts E and C. Let the glue dry.

9. Glue and screw parts B in place. Make sure that the corners are squared throughout; also measure the diagonals to be sure they are equal. Be generous with the glue because the glue needs to hold the gate together tightly to resist moisture.

10. Use a belt sander to sand smooth any unevenness on the cuts.

11. Attach the hinges and latch.

12. Place the post caps J on the posts.

Instructions for the fence
We recommend that you paint all the pieces before assembling them.

1. Set up the horizontal boards G with the corner brackets in the posts. Cut the top edge at an angle to allow water runoff.

2. Cut the points for the pickets H and then screw them in. Stretch a cord between the posts to make sure that all the pickets are the same height.

Sun gate & fence

Red and green are complementary colors, so, this red fence contrasts well with the greenery. The points are modeled after an old, classic example and fit well in the surroundings. Their shape is repeated in the caps of the gate posts. The large double gate with its two sunrise designs provides a happy and inviting impression and welcomes the home owners as well as visitors.

Materials for the gate

6 x 6 (5½ x 5½")
  2 pieces each 50"(A)
  2 pieces each 12" (E)

2 x 4 (1½ x 3½")
  2 pieces each 48" (F)
  4 pieces each 48" (G)
  2 pieces each 45" (H)
  2 pieces each 45" (I)
  2 pieces each 45" (J)
  2 pieces each 3.5" (K)

2 x 8 (1½ x 7½")
  2 pieces each 16" (L)

2 x 2 (1½ x 1½")(M), approx. 30'

Materials per fence section

4 x 4 (3½ x 3½"):
  1 piece 40" (B)

2 x 4 (1½ x 3½")
  2 pieces each 6' (C)

1 x 4 (¾ x 3½")
  13 pieces each 48" (D)

Additional materials

Plinths
Hexagonal bolts, washers,
  and nuts for the plinths
Gate hinges: 4
Gate latch
Wood dowel pins
Corner brackets for the fence
Screws
Glue for exterior use
Exterior paint

Instructions

It is a good idea to paint the wood all at once, before the final assembly, to protect the wood as the pieces are joined.

1. Set out the plinths (see page 105).

2. Attach posts A and B in the plinth post fasteners (see page 106). Make sure that the posts are vertical.

3. Screw the corner brackets securely to the horizontal rails C and then screw them in.

4. Profile cut the pickets D at the top with a jigsaw or band saw. Cut them at an angle on the lower end to allow water runoff. Attach a picket on each post B and then arrange the rest equally spaced, approx. ¾" apart.

5. Cut the tops for the gate posts E, 12" tall, from blocks the same dimensions as the posts. Use the same profile as for the pickets D and enlarge it to the width of the posts. Cut with a handsaw or, preferably, a band saw.

6. Glue and screw vertical boards F firmly to the gate posts.

7. Cut the uprights G and profile cut them at the top.

8. Cut the tenons for boards H, I, and J. The length and height of each tenon is 2" and the width ¾".

9. Mark the placement of the mortises for the tenons in the verticals G. Bore two holes with ¾" bore for each tenon and chisel out the hole with a sharp chisel.

10. Cut out the "sun" L with a radius of 8½". Join it to J with wood dowel pins and glue, clamp, and let glue dry.

11. Temporarily assemble pieces G, H, I, and J without glue. Measure the diagonals; if they are equal, the gate will be square.

12. Make sure the lengths of K are correct and cut them.

13. Measure, carefully mark, and then cut slats M by laying them in place and adjusting them until they fit. Begin with the center slat and then continue with those closer to the corner. There should be an angle of 18° between all the slats. Indicate on I, G, and L where the slats M will be attached.

14. Take the gate apart and bore the holes for the wood dowel pins.

15. Temporarily assemble the gate once more before the actual assembly, adjusting the pieces as necessary.

16. Firmly join all the parts with glue, clamp, and let glue dry. Use the glue generously because the glue not only holds the gate together, it also prevents water from running into any gaps.

17. Paint and finish the gate and gate posts.

Assemble the double gate as follows

1. Screw the gate hinges firmly to F.

2. Lay a 1"-thick board between the two halves of the gate and join them with clamps so they form a single piece. Wedge underneath so that they are precisely the same level and screw in the hinges. Remove the clamps and board and then open the gate.

3. Finish by attaching the gate latch.

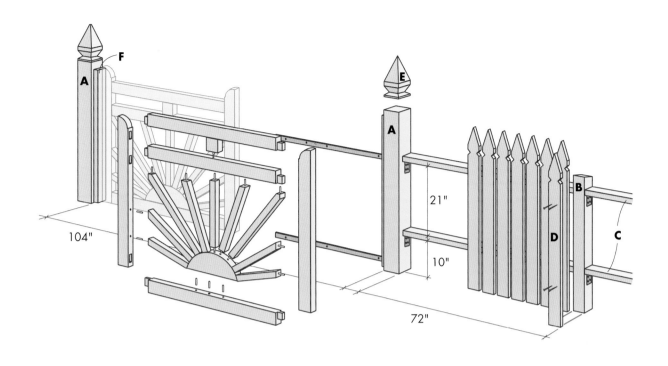

104"

21"

10"

72"

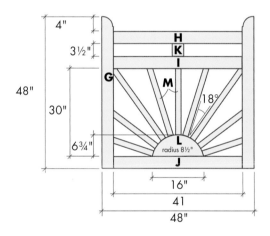

4"

3½"

48"

G

M

18°

30"

6¾"

radius 8½"

16"

41

48"

H
K
I
L
J

The job of making the caps for the gate posts is well worth the labor. The caps give the gate character and complete the look.

Double gate

When the gates are closed, they blend right into the fence, which makes a very nice and stylish whole. The effect is of a single, beautiful, white arched fence. The simple form fits perfectly with the early twentieth-century house, but it can also complement many different house styles, from the very old to modern contemporary.

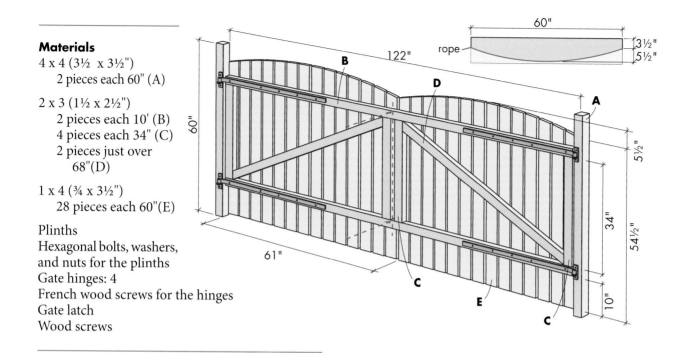

Materials

4 x 4 (3½ x 3½")
    2 pieces each 60" (A)

2 x 3 (1½ x 2½")
    2 pieces each 10' (B)
    4 pieces each 34" (C)
    2 pieces just over
        68"(D)

1 x 4 (¾ x 3½")
    28 pieces each 60"(E)

Plinths
Hexagonal bolts, washers,
and nuts for the plinths
Gate hinges: 4
French wood screws for the hinges
Gate latch
Wood screws

Instructions

Paint all the surfaces before the final assembly.

1. Bury the plinths (see page 105).

2. Attach posts A in the plinth post fasteners (see page 106). Make sure that the posts are vertical.

3. Cut the horizontal braces B and mount them between the posts with the hinges—check with a level. There should be a space of 1" to the gate posts on both sides.

4. Screw the uprights C in place, leaving a gap of ¾" between the two center pieces. Support the pieces under the center so that the gates don't sag during construction.

5. Clamp the diagonals D in place and mark where they should be cut. Remove them, cut them, and then set them in place. They should fit exactly and snugly when put in place. Screw them securely to all the uprights.

6. Screw in the fence boards E without trimming them. Stretch a cord between the posts at the bottom so you can place the fence boards all at the same height.

7. Make a template for the rounding of the gate. Using a masonite or plywood sheet, 60 x 9", attach a heavy rope or a chain so that it hangs down 5½" at the center (see insert drawing). Use this to draw the curve and then cut the template.

8. Place the template against horizontal B on one half of the gate, mark the rounding and then cut the fence boards with a jigsaw.

9. Cut horizontals B even with the two center upright supports C and open the gate!

10. Drive a screw through C and into the diagonal D in the four corners.

11. Attach the gate latch.

So that the gate posts can withstand the stress from the gate, you might need to set a wedged brace between the ground and the post on the inside (see fig. 11 on page 53).

Privacy fence
with doorway

For a privacy fence to be a bit less compact and have good proportions, we chose to build it at varying levels. The heights are adjusted for greater or lesser amounts of privacy at different places in the yard. The set-in doorway blends well with the fence, and the gaps between the fence boards effectively allow sunlight in.

Materials

4 x 4 (3½ x 3½")
   A = 76" (high)
   B = 62"
   (medium height)
   C = 50"(low)

2 x 4 (1½ x 3½")
   D = 84"
   J = 36"

1 x 4 (¾ x 3½")
   E = 68" (high)
   F = 54" (medium)
   G = 42" (low)
   K = 36"
   L = approx. 67"

Cut wood, 7/8 x 4 3/4":
   H = 84"
   H2 = 36"

Plinths
Hexagonal bolts, washers, and nuts for the plinths
Post caps (I). You can buy these ready-made at the lumberyard
Gate hinges: 4
Gate latch
Wood screws
optional: corner brackets

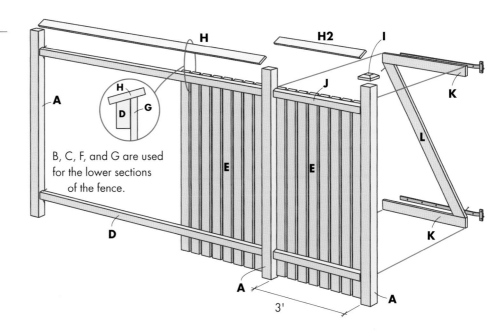

B, C, F, and G are used for the lower sections of the fence.

Instructions for the privacy fence

Don't forget to paint all the pieces before assembly.

1. Set out the plinths (see page 119).

2. Mount the posts A, B, and C in the plinths.

3. Cut horizontals D at a 15° angle along one long side (see the red circle on the drawing).

4. Join horizontals D to the posts. The easiest way is to use corner brackets on the posts, set up the boards, and screw them from underneath. On the privacy fence shown in the photos, the boards were joined by screwing diagonally into the posts. It is a bit more difficult, but you avoid having visible corner brackets. Use long screws and predrill and countersink so that the boards don't split at the ends.

5. Cut fence boards E, F, and G at a 15° angle on both ends to allow water runoff.

6. Screw the fence boards on securely. Begin with the two outermost boards and then the center board. Space the rest evenly so that the gap between

each is about ¾". Make sure everything is squared throughout by checking with a level. Stretch a cord 1½" from the lower edge of the posts so you can join the fence boards all at the same level.

7. Screw on the lintels H and the post caps I.

Instructions for the doorway

1. Cut the horizontal braces J as for D. Mount them temporarily with corner brackets. Note that both ends should be ¾" from the posts.

2. Join the fence boards E and the lintel H2 as for the privacy fence.

3. Screw the horizontal braces K on the inside of the door, centered on boards J.

4. Measure and cut the diagonal L very carefully, because its tight fit ensures that the door will hang straight rather than crooked. Securely screw on horizontal boards K and all the fence boards.

5. Mount the hangers on one post A and braces K. Remove the corner brackets and open the door.

Stable privacy fence

A long, high privacy fence must be constructed very well so that it will withstand the howling autumn winds. And it really couldn't be more stable than this! It takes a lot of lumber, but the fence will stand firm for many, many years. At the same time, this attractively shaped fence forms niches, like small rooms or planting spaces.

Materials

The materials list below is based on 2 posts for each section, but remember that added sections have 1 common post. All lumber should be pressure-treated.

60" Section
Posts, 4 x 4 (3½ x 3½")
 2 pieces each 96" (A)

Horizontal braces, 2 x 4 (1½ x 3½")
 3 pieces each 60" (B)

Vertical boards, 1 x 6 (¾ x 5½")
 9 pieces each 90" (C)

Horizontal trim, 1 x 5 (¾ x 4½")
 2 pieces each 60" (D)

Battens, 1 x 2 (¾ x 1½")
 10 pieces each 66" (F1),
  from which 2 pieces are ripped
  to 1¼" (E1)
 10 pieces each 15" (F2),
  from which 2 pieces are
  ripped to 1¼" (E2)

Covering boards, 1 x 6 (¾ x 5½")
 1 piece per post (at the outer
  corners, 2) each 96" (G)

Top boards, 1 x 5 (¾ x 4½")
 1 piece 60" (H)

30" Section
Posts, 4 x 4 (3½ x 3½")
 2 pieces each 96" (A)

Horizontal braces, 2 x 4 (1½ x 3½")
 3 pieces each 30" (B)

Vertical boards, 1 x 6 (¾ x 5½")
 5 pieces each 90" (C)

Horizontal trim, 1 x 5 (¾ x 4½")
 2 pieces each 30" (D)

Battens, 1 x 2 (¾ x 1½")
 6 pieces each 66" (F1),
  from which 2 pieces are ripped
  to 1¼" (E1)
 6 pieces each 15" (F2),
  from which 2 pieces are ripped
  to 1¼" (E2)

Covering boards, 1 x 6 (¾ x 5½")
 1 piece per post (at the outer
  corners, 2) each 96" (G)

Top boards, 1 x 5 (¾ x 4½")
 1 piece 30" (H)

Additional Materials
Plinths
Hexagonal bolts, washers,
 and nuts for the plinths
Wood screws
Corner brackets, 1¾" wide:
 2 pieces per board B
Post caps (I): 1 for each post A

Instructions

1. Set out the plinths (see page 105).

2. Set the posts A carefully (see page 52).

3. Screw the corner brackets to horizontal braces B and firmly screw on the boards.

4. Screw on the vertical boards C, spacing them equidistantly. The vertical boards should be cut at an angle at the lower ends to allow water runoff.

5. Screw on the horizontal trim D.

6. The battens E1 & E2 should be ripped to 1¼". Cut the battens E2 with an angle at the lower ends to allow water runoff. Screw the battens E1 & E2 securely to the posts with the wide side against the post so that the batten reaches the edge (see fig. inside the red circle).

7. Screw on the covering battens F. Cut the battens F2 at an angle at the lower edge to allow water runoff.

8. Securely screw the covering boards G to the posts. At the outer corner one should be split to 4¾" wide.

9. Screw top boards H on firmly.

10. The post caps I on this privacy fence are poured concrete, but you can also make them out of wood. One alternative is to cut the posts diagonally at the top and screw in a block board ¾ x 5½ x 5½".

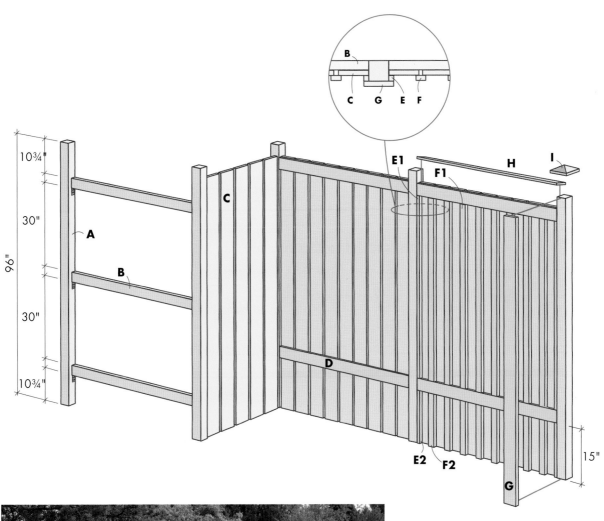

10¾"

30"

96"

30"

10¾"

A

B

C

B

C G E F

E1

F1

H

I

D

E2 F2

G

15"

The niches make it possible to create various small spaces in the yard. Let your imagination run wild!

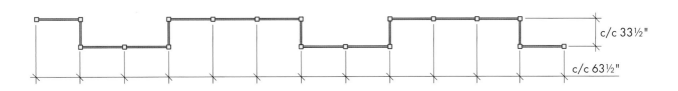

c/c 33½"

c/c 63½"

69

Wind break

This privacy fence constructed with pressure-treated lumber provides protection from the wind and onlookers. With its modern design, this shelter is also a pretty garden feature that frames an outdoor area. The large, green plants next to it complete the "room" in the yard in a soft and inviting way.

Materials

Pressure-treated lumber,
    4 x 4 (3½ x 3½")
        3 pieces each 6' (A)

    1 x 4 (¾ x 3½")
        3 pieces each 64½" (B)
        3 pieces each 62¼" (C)
        3 pieces each 60" (D)
        3 pieces each 59¼" (E)

    2 x 2 (1½ x 1½")
        46 pieces each 67¾" (F)

Plinths: 3
Hexagonal bolts, washers, and nuts for the plinths
Wood screws

Instructions

1. Bury the plinths (see page 105).

2. Cut the posts A with a 45° angle at the top.

3. Set the posts in place with the fasteners on the plinths, checking to make sure they are straight with a level, and then screw them in with the hexagonal bolts, washers, and nuts.

4. Cut the pieces B, C, D, and E. If the posts are not arranged exactly as in the drawing, adjust the measurements.

5. Screw horizontal braces B firmly to the posts and then join horizontal braces C to one of the posts A and into board B.

6. Cut the fence boards F with a 45° angle at the top.

7. Screw the two outer fence boards F firmly in from the front side on both sections.

8. Arrange the remaining 22 fence boards for each section with approx. ¾" space between each. Screw them on from the back.

9. Screw on braces D and E.

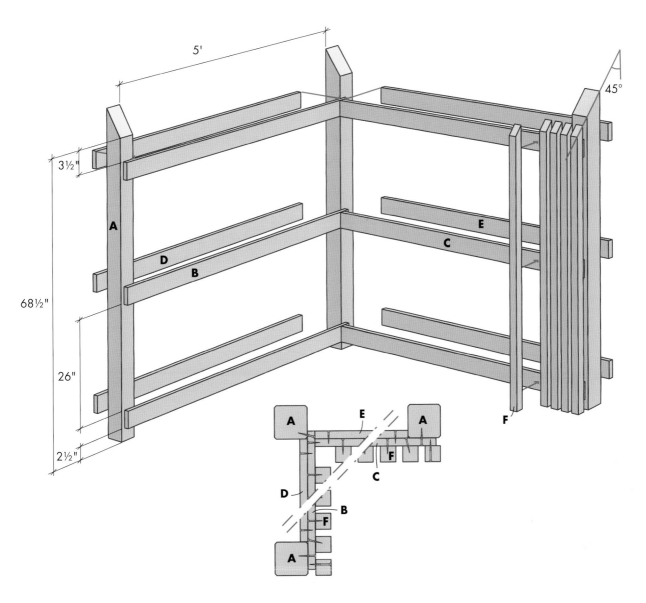

5'

3½"

68½"

26"

2½"

45°

A

D

B

E

C

F

A · E · A

D · C · F

B

F

A

The fence is the same design as the wind break.

Outdoor
"room" divider

We want to call it a room divider—a fence that frames in the garden space. This one was constructed in various forms, so, to unify it, was painted the same shade of red as the old wooden barn and the aluminum strips on the greenhouse. By varying the shapes, you get exciting and different fencing solutions, with a privacy fence for outdoor protection and an open fence and gate offering a welcoming view in. Sitting on one of the posts, a little surprisingly, is a matching birdhouse.

Privacy fence

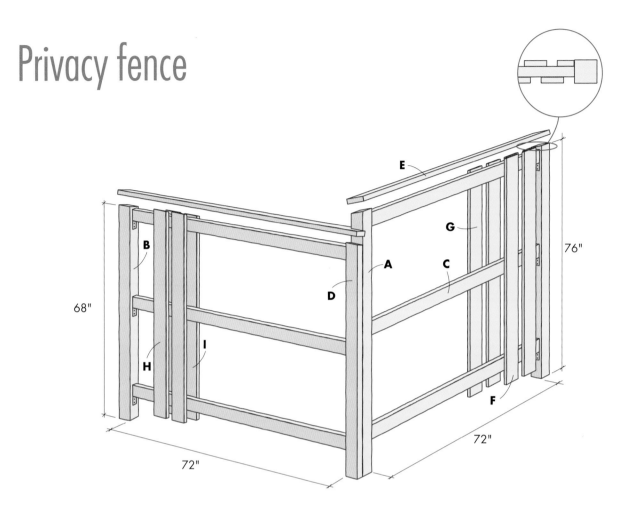

Materials

Posts, 4 x 4 (3½ x 3½")
    2 pieces each 76"+ (A)
    1 piece 68" (B)

2 x 4 (1½ x 3½")
    6 pieces each 72" (C)

1 x 4 (¾ x 3½")
    1 piece 68" (D)

2 x 6 (1½ x 5½")
    2 pieces, each 80" (E)

Cut wood, 1 x 4'":
    14 pieces each 73" (F)
    13 pieces each 71⅝" (G)
    14 pieces each 65" (H)
    13 pieces each 63⅝" (I)

Poured plinths (see page 106).
Hexagonal bolts, washers,
    and nuts for the plinths
Construction brackets
Wood screws
Nails

*The best shelter one
gets from a privacy
fence is that it averts
some of the wind.*

Instructions

1. Bury the plinths (see page 106).

2. Cut posts A and B a little longer than the measurements given in the Materials list.

3. Level and mount the posts A and B in the plinth fasteners using the hexagonal bolts, nuts, and washers. Use a level to make sure that the posts are vertical.

4. Cut horizontal braces C. Measure the distance between the posts and cut them as precisely as possible. Mount them centered on the posts with the construction brackets and screws.

   At the place where the boards on the lower section meet the corner post, they should not be centered but mounted flush with the edge of the post A.

5. Cut the top of the posts to the correct height with a 20° upwards angle.

6. Cut and nail the covering board D that sits on the post at the corner. This board should also be cut with a 20° angle at the top. Cut at an angle at the bottom so that the board has a so-called "drop nose."

7. Cut and nail in the lintels E. Note that the ends will extend about ½" beyond the posts.

8. Cut the covering boards F–I. Note that the inside boards should be 1⅜" shorter than those on the outside. Cut them with a 20° angle at the top. Cut them diagonally at the bottom to allow water runoff.

9. Paint the posts, horizontals, lintels, as well as the inside, edges, and ends of the wood on both ends of the covering boards before these are assembled.

10. Nail the covering boards into place with the core side facing outwards. Space them evenly apart.

Fence

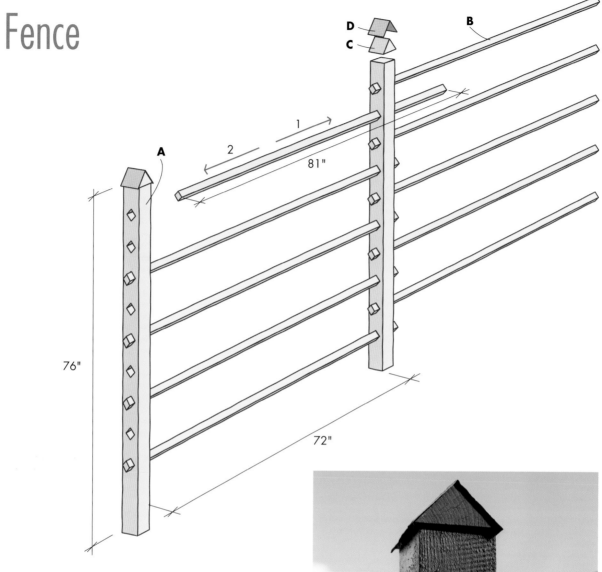

A 76"
B
C
D
1
2
81"
72"

Materials

Posts 4 x 4 (3½ x 3½") (A):
   76" per post

Rails, 2 x 2 (1¾ x 1¾") (B):
   81 x 5 pieces per section

Shaped lumber (triangular), 4 x 4 (3½ x 3½") (C):
   5" length per post cut diagonally

Plinths
Hexagonal bolts, washers, and nuts for the plinths
Sheet metal (D) for the post cap
Nails

A little roof on top of the fence post protects the wood from moisture.

Instructions

1. Dig the holes for the plinths and then set out the prepared plinths (see page 105).

2. Cut posts A to the correct length.

3. Measure and draw the placement of the square holes for the rails B. The fence shown in the photo here stands on a slight slope; on even ground there should be 4 rails in every other section. Bore the holes and chisel them until square.

4. Level and mount the posts in the plinth fasteners using the hexagonal bolts, washers, and nuts. Use a level to make sure the posts are vertical. Also make sure that the square holes align horizontally with each other.

5. Cut the horizontal rails B and set them into place by pounding them into the holes. Nail them into position.

6. Cut the triangular blocks C for the post caps. Nail them into place. Cut and bend pieces of the sheet metal D for each post and nail into place.

A mixture of fence and rail.
Open, simple, and stylish!

Gate

Materials

Posts, 4 x4 (3½ x 3½")
    2 pieces each 76" (A)

2 x 4 (1½ x 3½")
    1 piece 48" (B)

Shaped lumber (triangular), 4 x 4 (3½ X 3½")
    1 piece 50" long, cut diagonally (C)

Sheet metal for the roof:
    1 piece 51 x 8" (D)

2 x 3 (1½ x 2½")
    2 pieces each 35" (E)

Rails, 1 x 1 (¾ x ¾")
    10 pieces each 54" (F)

Plinths
Hexagonal bolts, nuts,
    and washers for the plinths
Long hinges (G): 2
Stainless steel pins
Nails

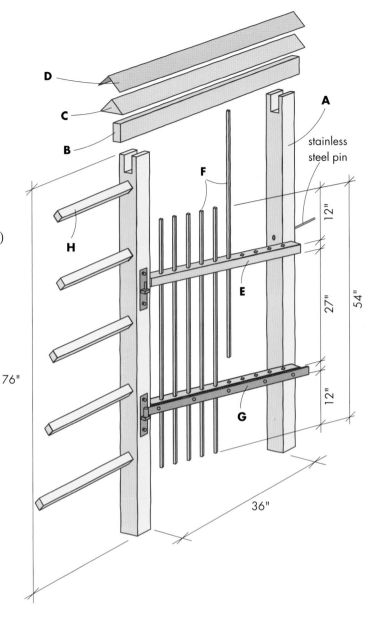

Instructions

1. Dig the holes for the plinths and then set out the prepared plinths (see page 105).

2. Cut posts A to the correct length (if they are not part of a fence and already in place). Cut and chisel out the notches for the top board B. Bore and chisel out square holes for the fence rails H, if you are making that type of fence.

3. Level and mount the posts A in the plinth fasteners with hexagonal bolts, nuts, and washers. Use a level to make sure that the posts are vertical. Also make sure that the square holes for the fence rails H are aligned horizontally with the corresponding holes in the fence posts.

The hinge stretches all the way along the board and sticks out a bit. This extended piece functions as a stop against the post.

The pin holds the gate closed—a simple way to lock a gate that should be used more often.

4. Cut the lintel (B) and the shaped lumber (C) and attach them with glue and nails. Bend the plates (D) and nail them over board (C).

5. Cut boards E for the gate. Measure and mark the placement of the 10 F rails. Bore using a ⅝" bore and chisel out the square holes.

6. Cut the rails F and press them into the boards. They should fit snugly, so pound them in with a mallet. Secure the rails with nails.

7. Mount the hinges G and cut them so they extend about 2" beyond the boards. Hang the gate, close it and bore a hole through the post and into the end wood of the top board E. Hammer in a stainless steel pin as a simple latch.

Birdhouse

A birdhouse sits on one of the fence posts. The size of the base is determined by the dimensions of the post. In this case, the bottom is 4 x 4". The inside should always be rough-sawn wood to make it easier for the birds to get into the entry hole.

The birdhouse in the picture has a perch. It looks nice, but if there are any predator birds or other predatory animals in the neighborhood who could use the perch to get at the birds, then you should omit it. It is also a good idea to nail tacks all around the hole or to nail a plate to the birdhouse to prevent the birds' enemies from being able to get into the hole.

To clean the birdhouse, you just have to lift it up and then you can clean the top of the post.

Instructions

1. Dig the holes for the plinths and then set out the prepared plinths (see page 105).

2. Cut post A to the correct length (if it is not part of a fence and already in place

3. Level and mount the post A in the plinth fasteners with hexagonal bolts, nuts, and washers. Use a level to make sure that the post is vertical.

4. Cut the front B and the back C. The peak is a 45° angle and the sides angle in at 67.5°. Bore a hole using a 1" diameter bore in the front approx. 15" from the bottom.

5. Cut the sides D. Cut the top parts of these so that they follow the slope of B and C, 67.5°.

6. Glue and nail parts B, C, and D together.

7. Cut the pieces for roof E, which has four parts that are glued together in pairs. Clamp them and let dry. The bevel cut at the peak should be 22.5°.

8. Glue and nail the roof onto the birdhouse. Bend plate F and nail it into place.

9. Push the birdhouse onto the post. If it is a tight fit, sand the post lightly until the birdhouse slides into place easily. It should slide down about 10".

10. When the birdhouse is at the right height, hammer 2 nails into each side of the post for it to rest on.

The birdhouse can be part of the fence as shown here or have its own post.

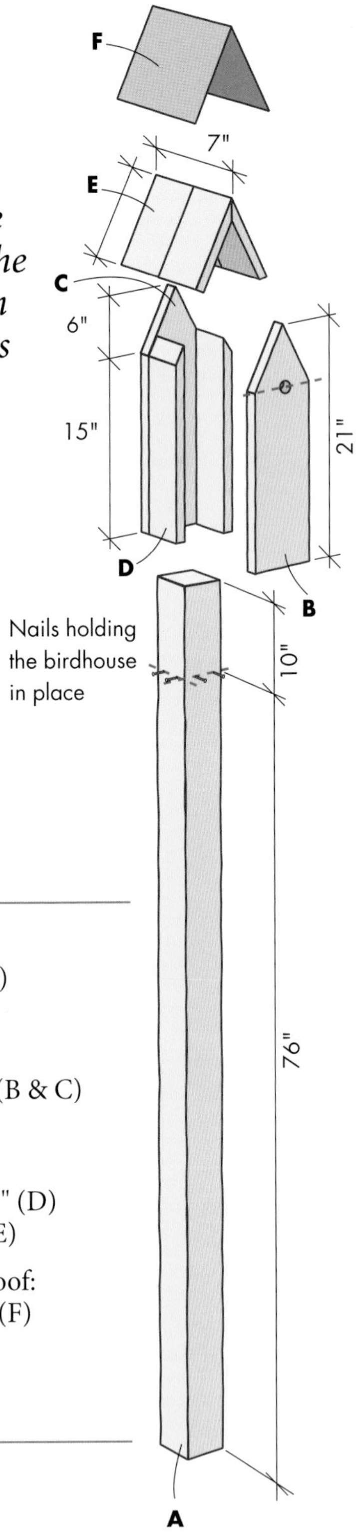

Nails holding the birdhouse in place

Materials
Post, 4 x 4 (3½ x 3½")
   1 piece 76" (A)

1 x 6 (¾ x 5½")
   2 pieces each 21" (B & C)
   ripped to 5" wide

1 x 4 (¾ x 3½")
   2 pieces each 15¾" (D)
   4 pieces each 8" (E)

Sheet metal for the roof:
   1 piece 7" x 16½" (F)

Glue for exterior use
Nails

For play and pleasure

If you don't feel ready to build a fence or a deck, maybe you can start with some smaller, simpler projects. Why not make a bird feeder, a birdhouse, or a table for the balcony? Or what about some play equipment for the children? Maybe an outdoor shower for the family? It's not hard and absolutely not expensive. Just get going. The instruction in the book will help get you on the way.

Play equipment

When you are constructing play equipment, you have to consider safety.
• Oversize the materials to minimize the risk of breaking and binding from stress.
• Round off the edges wherever there is a risk that the children can hurt themselves.
• Sand all the surfaces that anyone can grasp to minimize the risk for splinters or wrap rope or strips of leather around those places.
• Make sure that all screws are properly countersunk.
• Check all the playthings regularly.

Birdhouses

Building a birdhouse certainly isn't difficult, but there are some things to take into consideration. Here are a few tips about the design and measurements for some of our most common small birds.
• Make sure that the size of the birdhouse and its design is suitable for the birds you want to have living in it.
• Use pine and turn the rough-sawn side to the inside so that the birds can cling to the surface with their claws when they want to go out.
• The inside of the birdhouse should not be painted or made with treated materials.
• The outside should be coated with water-based paint.
• Do not paint the entry hole. Instead, bore the hole diagonally upwards to prevent rainwater from running into the nest.
• Use galvanized or rustproof screws for the joins.
• Make sure that the birdhouse is cleaned after the birds have fledged.

• Avoid a perch on the birdhouse, because it can make it easier for predators to get in.
• The birdhouse can be used by birds for sleeping at night during the winter. For that reason, don't use wood that is too thin.
• Avoid nailing the birdhouse up because it can damage the tree. Instead, set it up with a wire around the tree or by attaching a transverse board to the birdhouse and securing it between two branches.

The table below shows suggested birdhouse sizes for some of the most common small birds.

Bird species	Starling (also house sparrow and nuthatch)	Titmouse (also flycatcher and tree sparrow)
Bottom, inches	4¾ x 5⅞	4 x 5⅛
Internal height front/back, inches	11¾/ 13¾	7⅞ / 9⅞
Entry hole, diameter in inches	2	1⅛
Measurement from hole to bottom, inches	9⅞	5⅞

You can find instructions for birdhouses on pages 82 and 89.

Balcony table

A little corner shelf you can simply hang over the edge of the railing for an attractive detail that works on a small, as well as a large, balcony. The table is spray painted with high-gloss red paint that looks good and is especially effective against the black iron railings.

Materials

The measurements of the balcony table should be adjusted to fit the width and thickness of the balcony railing. The table shown here was made for a balcony rail 1½" thick. Parts C and D were determined by the length. Parts E and F were calculated on both the length and the width.

½" plywood:
    15 x 8¼" (A)
    15½ x 8¼" (B)
    17½ x 2½" (C)
    18 x 2½" (D)
    18 x 2½" (E and F)
    15 x 15" (G)

Glue for exterior use
Wood screws
Exterior paint

Instructions

1. Cut all of the pieces. G has a radius of 17" and the sides are 15"; the center lies outside the piece. E and F are cut at a 45° angle at one end.

2. Glue and screw the parts together in the following order. Don't forget to counterbore.
• Join A and B
• Join G securely to A and B
• Join E and F
• Finally, join C and D, which are also screwed together.

3. Be very careful with the finishing. Begin by oiling the ends of the wood, and then apply two coats of primer before painting.

A lovely interlude on the balcony— tea time with a good book.

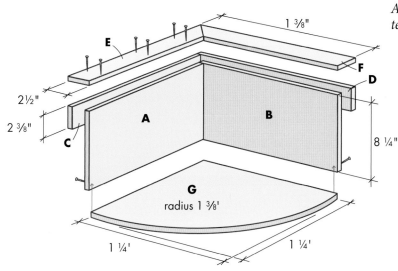

Bird feeder & birdhouse

A little red house with white gables and roofing felt for all of the small overwintering birds. They can sit comfortably on the round rails; suet balls hang underneath. A truly fine feeder.

Materials for the bird feeder

¼" plywood
  1 piece 10 x 5" (A)
  2 pieces each 7 x 8½" (E)
  2 pieces each 7 x 3½" (G)
  1 piece 6 x 12" (H1)
  1 piece 6¼ x 12" (H2)

Pine molding, approx. ½ x 1¼"
  2 pieces each 10" (B)
  2 pieces each 8½" (C)
  1 piece 9½" (F)

Dowels, ½" diameter
  2 pieces each 11¾" (D)
  4 pieces each 2¾" (K)

Pine molding, approx. ¼ x 1":
  4 pieces each 6¾" (I)

Pressure-treated post, 4 x 4 (3½ x 3½"):
  approx. 84" (J)

Plexiglas, ⅛" thick:
  2 pieces each 9¾ x 6"

Asphalt roofing felt: 1 piece 12 x 12½"
Roofing felt adhesive
Glue for exterior use
Wood screws
Wire nails

Instructions for the bird feeder

1. Glue and nail strips B securely to the bottom A with thin wood nails.

2. Bore ½" holes in the gable strips C and trim the dowels D. Attach the dowels to C with glue and wire nails. Glue and nail C into A and B.

3. Cut the gables E (the angle at the top is 90º). Cut using a circular saw or router, cut ⅛" grooves, ⅛" deep in E for the Plexiglas. The groove should be 1" in from the edge. Glue and screw the gables E to C.

4. Glue and screw the roof beam F into gables E. Counterbore for the screws.

5. Glue and nail together the roof gables G with roof boards H1 and H2. Make sure that the roof gables G are 10" apart on the inside and fit over gables E.

6. Cut the roof wind boards I at a 45º angle, counterbore and attach them firmly with glue and wire nails.

7. Cut the Plexiglas sheets with a fine-toothed saw. Cut the notches at the lower edge. The notches should be 7½ x 1".

8. Cut the roofing felt and glue it down well, carefully heating the felt when you fold it so it will be easier for the felt to adhere tightly.

9. Shape the point of post J. Bore 4 holes (½" diameter) approx. 4" down on the post, glue and push in the four dowels K.

10. Firmly screw on the birdfeeder with large screws through the base A and down onto the post J.

It is much easier if you prime and paint all the parts before the final assembly.

Materials for the birdhouse

1 x 6 (¾ x 5½") Rough-sawn wood is best:
    1 piece 15" (A)
    1 piece 10" (C)
    1 piece 8" (E)

1 x 6 (¾ x 5½"):
    2 pieces each 12" (B)
    1 piece 4" (F)

1 x 1 (¾ x ¾"):
    2 pieces each 4" (D)

Nails
Wire

Instructions for the birdhouse

Face the rough-sawn side of the wood to the inside on all parts.

1. Cut the back A the correct length. Bore 2 holes ¾" from the top. Nail support D, centered from the sides, 1" from the bottom.

2. Cut the pieces for the sides B and nail them securely to the back A.

3. Cut the front C, noting the angle at the top edge. Nail rail D to the lower edge, centered from the sides.

4. Bore an entry hole, 1¼" diameter, with the center 8" from the lower edge of C.

5. Nail the front C firmly to the sides B.

6. Cut the roof E, noting the angle at the back edge, and then nail it on securely.

7. Cut the base F so that it is 4 x 5½" and then push it in from below and let it rest on supports D. Make sure that the base isn't too big; if it is, the house can be too drafty. It is easy to remove the base from the bottom so that the birdhouse can be cleaned.

8. Thread a wire through the holes in the back A and hang the birdhouse around a tree.

With a bird feeder and a birdhouse, you can have small birds in your yard all year.

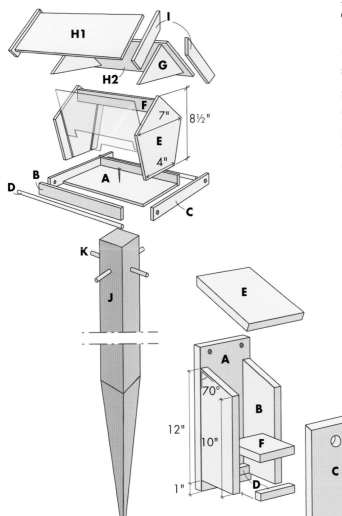

89

Soccer goal

A soccer goal is one of the most fantastic playthings you can make for your children. They can have a lot of fun playing with their friends or an adult can be the goalkeeper when the children need to practice kicking "real smokers." The goal is very stable and remains standing even when post-shot and crossbar hits whizz past your ears. If you prefer handball, this goal works just as well.

Materials

2 x 3 (1½ x 2½"):
    2 pieces each 60" (A)
    2 pieces each 68" (B and F)
    2 pieces each 5" (C)
    2 pieces each 67½" (D)
    2 pieces each 30½" (E)

Carriage bolts with washers
    and nuts: 2
Hexagonal bolts with washers
    and wing nuts: 2
Hinges: 2
Corner brackets: 2
Wood screws
Glue for exterior use
Exterior paint
Soccer netting: 144 x
    72". For safety,
    choose a net with 4" mesh.
Staples
Hooks

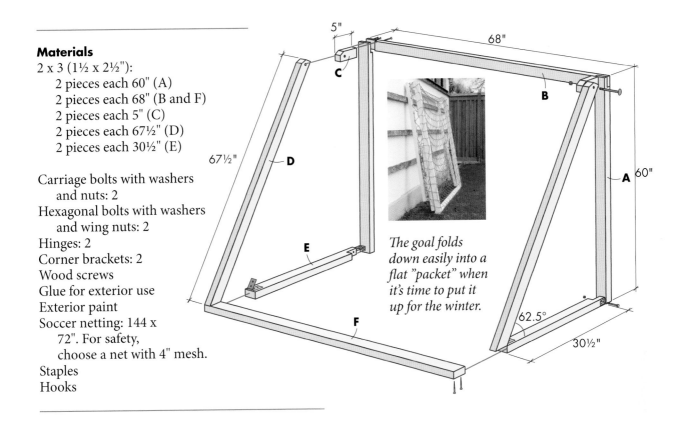

The goal folds down easily into a flat "packet" when it's time to put it up for the winter.

Instructions

1. Cut posts A and the crossbar B. Glue and screw them together with lap joints.

2. Cut two support rails C and glue and screw them securely at the top corners 1½" in from the side.

3. Cut the diagonals D, making them a little bit longer than shown in the drawing. Cut one end at a 62.5° angle.

4. Cut the side rails E. Cut a notch on the inside at the goalpost end. The notches are made so the wing nuts can be countersunk and no one can be injured by them.

5. Join siderails E and the diagonals D with the hinges.

6. Cut the back bar F, glue and screw it firmly to the diagonals D.

7. Screw the construction brackets securely to the lower end of the back side of posts A. The inside of the corner brackets should align with the outside of the posts. Set the pieces in place so that E abuts the brackets; mark placement of the holes and bore. Screw the parts together with the hexagonal bolts, wing nuts, and washers.

8. Clamp the diagonals D to the support rails C. Make sure that the goal is straight all around. Bore the holes for the carriage bolts and then join C and D securely with the bolts.

9. Draw a line where the diagonals D should be trimmed. Disassemble, trim, and bevel off the top corner. Also bevel the corner on C.

10. Paint the entire construction.

11. Assemble the goal. Staple the netting on well but not too tightly or the ball will rebound. Do not attach the netting along the bottom to E or you won't be able to fold down the goal. Instead, screw in some hooks that the net can catch in.

Netting for soccer goals can be a little hard to find but you can buy it over the internet.

Garden shower

Summer, sun, and warmth! Water is needed then. When the size of the lot or perhaps your budget puts a stop to the dream of a tiled swimming pool, the garden shower is an excellent alternative.

This one is constructed with pressure-treated wood and has the simplest and cheapest solution for the water source: a common garden hose. A great way to cool down on a hot summer day!

Materials

Pressure-treated lumber, 2 x 4 (1½ x 3½")
   1 piece 26" (A)
   3 pieces each 23" (B and C)
   2 pieces each 21½" (D)
   2 pieces each 10¾"(E)
   1 piece 72" (F)

Pressure-treated decking, 5/4 x 4 (1 x 3½")
   2 pieces each 74" (G)
   7 pieces each 27" (H)

Wood screws
Glue for exterior use
Hexagonal bolts, nuts, and washers
Shower fixtures and water faucet

Instructions

1. Cut pieces A–E for the base frame. Glue and screw the pieces together. It is important that the E pieces are placed close enough together that a 3½" wide board just fits between them.

2. Cut vertical F (72" long) and cut it at a 45° angle 36" from one end.

3. Cut the two uprights G and make a 1½ x 3½" notch on one end as shown in the drawing.

4. Glue and screw boards F and G to form a post.

5. Set the post in place on the base frame, bore, and then join it very firmly with hexagonal bolts, nuts, and washers.

6. Cut the decking boards H. Cut a 2" deep x 5½" wide notch for the post in one of them.

7. Securely screw the decking boards to the base frame. Note that they should extend out ½" on all sides of the base frame. Begin with the two outermost boards and then space the remaining boards evenly across.

8. Oil all the wood, and, most importantly, the wood ends.

9. Assemble the faucet and shower fixtures, add on the hose, and take a shower.

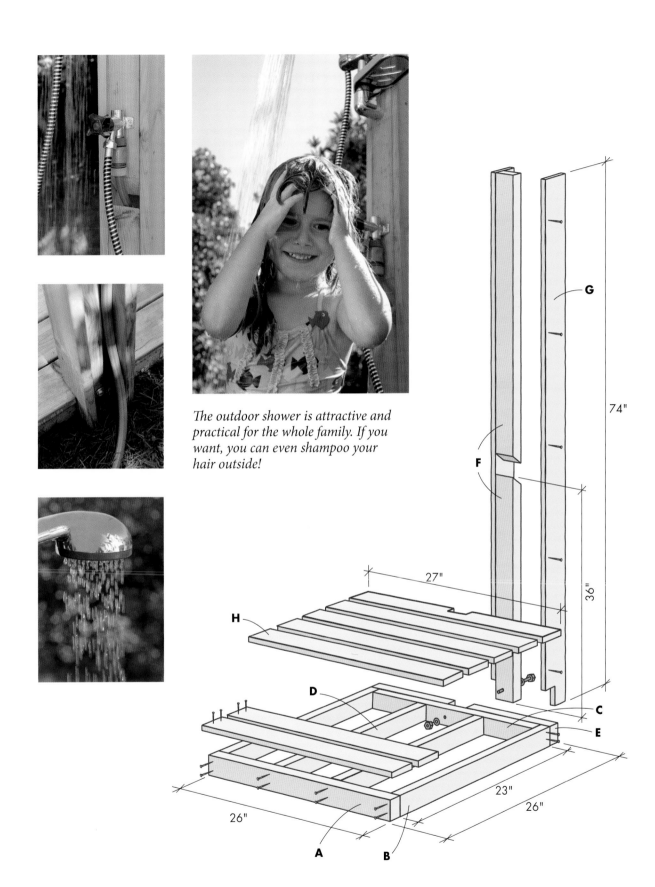

The outdoor shower is attractive and practical for the whole family. If you want, you can even shampoo your hair outside!

74"

36"

27"

23"

26"

26"

G

F

H

D

E

C

A

B

Skateboard ramp

Children can hang out with their friends here, practice their jumps, and discover some new tricks. The skateboard ramp requires a bit of space, but what a "plaything!" When the construction was ready, we bought several cans of spray paint and let the kids decorate the ramp.

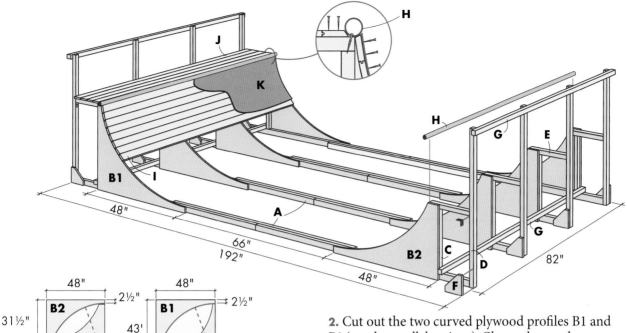

Materials

¾" plywood
   2 sheets each 48 x 96" (B1, B2, and F)

2 x 3 (1½ x 2½")
   12 pieces, each 96" (A)

2 x 2 (1½ x 1½")
   4 pieces each 27½" and 4 pieces each 39" (C)
   8 pieces each 67" (D)
   8 pieces each 22" (E)
   4 pieces each 82" (G)

Unfinished tongue-and-groove, 1 x 4 (¾ x 3½")
   62 pieces each 82" (I and J)

2" galvanized pipe, (2⅜" diameter)
   2 pieces each 82" (H)

Tempered board (Masonite), ⅛":
   4 sheets each 4 x 8" (K)

Corner brackets: 8
Wood screws
Glue for exterior use

Instructions

Prepare a flat surface, preferably so that the ramp can sit on stones. It is a good idea to paint all the pieces before assembly.

1. Screw boards A together three-by-three (two end-to-end with one overlapping the joint).

2. Cut out the two curved plywood profiles B1 and B2 (see the small drawings). Glue and securely screw them to boards A, 13¾" from the ends of A.

3. Glue and screw the standing boards C to B1 and B2. Note that B1 and B2 have different height measurements.

4. Cut out parts F (approx. 8 x 8"), nail and glue A and D with them, being careful with the corners.

5. Now the frames are finished. Raise them and screw and glue them together with boards G (2 pieces on each side).

6. Join boards E to D with the corner brackets, and glue and screw E to B, at the same time. Trim the E pieces so that they don't extend beyond B.

7. Bore holes in pipe H. First bore through both pipe walls with a bore that is a tiny bit larger than the screws. Next, bore the hole in one wall of the pipe so that the screws can go through. Screw the pipe in securely. Hold pieces of the skating ramp against the pipe so that it has the correct placement.

8. Screw the tongue-and-groove I into place. The first, directly below the pipe H, is cut diagonally so it will support the pipe. Counterbore the holes for all the screws.

9. Screw the tongue-and-groove J in. The board that lies against the pipe H should be cut diagonally to support the pipe well.

10. Screw board K in place and then clean-cut the edges. Hardboard is susceptible to weather. In Europe they have an oil treated hardboard that is weather resistant. Lacking that, treat the hardboard with a good spar urethane or other weather-resistant coating. In the photo you can see how the leftover pieces of plywood have been screwed onto the railing as decoration.

Piers

Not everyone is lucky enough to own a waterside lot. So, we congratulate you if you are one of those who have the opportunity to build your own pier. Your boat can bob and gurgle in the waves, and the adventurous can take a dip in the cool summer waters. The pier is also a lovely gathering place for sun bathers. For anyone who likes to fish, the pier will be a fine new fishing spot, with fish lured into the shadows beneath the pier's boards. Leaf through the following pages and find inspiration!

A pier is a multi-use construction. It can be a place to tie up your boat or the swimming pier you've always wanted. Maybe it will serve as an extra outdoor area where you can relax with friends and enjoy a lovely summer evening. No matter how the pier is used, it will eventually be worn down by water, ice, weather, and wind. It is very important to take all these factors into consideration from the very beginning so you can construct it in the right place.

There are also a number of other factors to consider before building your pier.

Planning

Consider the general and particular aspects of the area and if they can be affected by the pier. These include the environment of the water, fishing, bird life, and much more. If the pier affects any of these general or particular aspects, it may have certain conditions placed on it. Consult your municipal authorities so they can help you decide about the pier building from all aspects.

Talk with neighbors—perhaps you can build a pier to share. Be sure you get permission from the land owner and anyone holding water rights.

You may need governmental permission to build a pier. Contact the local building permits office for more information.

There are several types of piers. The most common are piers built on posts, free-floating piers, overhung piers, and those built on stone. Which type is most suitable depends on where the pier will be constructed. Every community has its traditions that you should take into consideration.

Special marine-grade, pressure-treated wood protects against shipworm in salt and fresh water. Check with your supplier to find which type is best for your application. Any metal pieces should be galvanized or completely rustproof. Further north, you need to remember that the ice can become quite thick and last a long time.

A pier built on posts

This type of pier is appropriate for gravel, sand, or mud beds that are easy to sink the posts in.

Materials
Posts: A = 4 x 4 (3½ x 3½")

Cut wood:
    B = 2 x 6 (1½ x 5½")1½ x 4⅞"
    C and D = 2 x 4 (1½ x 3½")
    E = 2 x 6 (1½ x 5½")

Decking wood:
    F = 5/4 x 6 (1 x 5½")

Wood screws and nails

Instructions
1. If possible, dig out the holes in the bed for the posts A.

2. Carve one end of A to a point and then sink the posts with, for example, a sledgehammer, going down as far as possible. The distance between the pairs of posts should be a maximum of 6'.

3. Connect the posts in pairs with the crosspieces B.

4. Reinforce the structure with cross C: First assemble one crossbar and the spacing block D. Then attach the second crossbar on the spacing block, centering it on the first crossbar.

5. Nail or screw in the beams E, screwing diagonally on the center beam. Beams should be a minimum of 16" on center.

6. Screw the decking boards F down the pier.

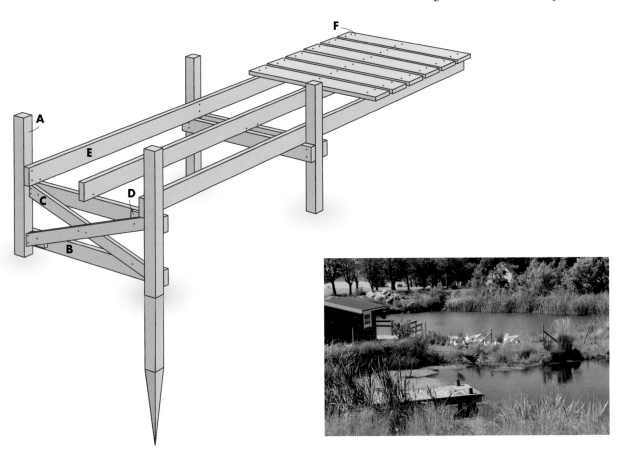

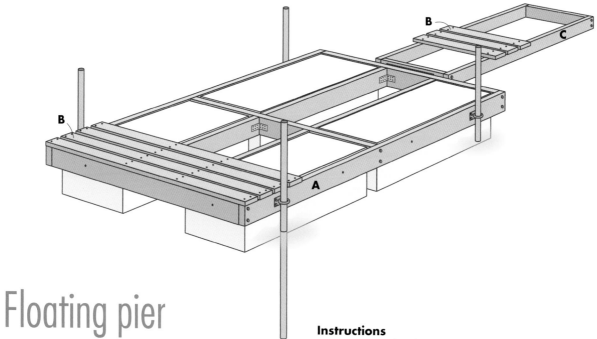

Floating pier

A floating pier follows the changes in the water level and is easy to remove for winter storage.

There are many types and sizes of floating blocks or billets on the market. For this pier, we've used foam billets specifically made for this purpose. This type of billet has minimal water absorption. They come in a variety of sizes. For this dock the billets are 48 x 20 x 15". You can buy or order foam blocks at a building supply store and get the size you need.

The total measurements of the pier are 60 x 100½". The gangway is 30" wide.

Materials
Floating blocks: 4

Cut wood:
    A = 2 x 6 (1½ x 5½")
    C = 2 x 4 (1½ x 3½")

Decking wood: B = 2 x 6 (1½ x 5½")

Galvanized pipes, 2" diameter
Anchoring eye bolts for 2-inch pipe
Gangway coupling
Hexagonal bolts, washers, and nuts
French wood screws
Corner brackets
Wood screws

Instructions

1. Measure the floating blocks you have, adding approx. ¾" to the length and width. These are the inner measurements of the compartments that will hold the floating blocks. The center compartment, which will not contain any blocks, should be somewhat narrower than the filled compartments (in this case they are 14").

2. Cut the pieces for the frame A and screw them together with French wood screws and with construction brackets and anchor screws.

3. Attach the anchoring eye bolts and the part of the gangway coupling that will connect to the pier with bolts, nuts, and washers that go all the way through.

4. Set the blocks in and fix them with a few long screws through the planks and into the blocks.

5. Firmly screw in the decking boards.

6. Put the pier in the water and hammer in the pipes.

7. Cut the pieces for the gangway frame C; the short bars are 25" long. Make sure that the long boards reach an appropriate place on the beach. Screw the frame together with the French wood screws and assemble the section of the gangway coupling that will connect to the gangway with through bolts, washers, and nuts.

8. Attach decking boards B, 30" long, for the gangway with screws.

9. Join the pier and the gangway.

Overhanging pier

If you have a beach with sloping cliffs, and the pier won't be too long, this is an appropriate type of pier. You don't have to worry about the pier being damaged by ice or varying water levels.

Materials

The distance between the foundation and the pier built on it is approx. 3' and the total length of the pier is approximately 10'.

Cut wood:
    A = 2 x 6 (1½ x 5½")
    B = 2 x 8 (1½ x 7½")
    C = 2 x 6 (1½ x 5½")

Decking wood: D = 2 x 6 (1½ x 5½")

Expanding grout, threaded rods, and nuts
Concrete
Roofing underlayment
Corner brackets: 3
Wood screws

Instructions

1. Bore the holes in the rock with a bore hammer for rock boring (you can rent this equipment). Attach the threaded rods with expanding grout to the holes in the rock.

2. Cast the concrete foundation in a simple shape around the threaded rods. The outer foundation block should be 1½" lower than the inner one.

3. Screw boards A to the outer foundation, laying roofing underlayment between the concrete and the wood.

4. Lay out the beams B. Join them to the inner foundation with board C, which is attached with threaded rods and nuts. Lay the roofing underlayment between the beams and the concrete foundation. Note that you shouldn't bore through the beams for the threaded rods which should lie with a maximum of 16" on center. Finally, attach the beams to the outer foundation with corner brackets.

5. Attach the decking boards D with screws.

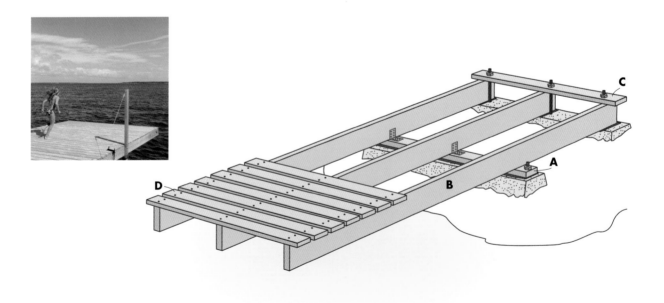

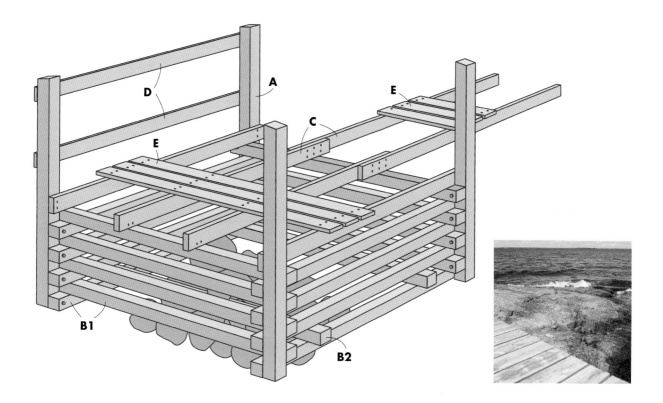

Pier with stone foundation

This pier is an alternative when the bed isn't suitable for sinking down posts. It can often be built on land and then rolled out and filled with stones. A pier with a stone caisson is a sturdy construction resistant to ice damage. Formerly, people used to build these structures on the ice and then hack away the ice so that the caisson sunk at the right place, a risky method that should be used only with the greatest caution.

The outer measurements of the caisson are 72 x 72". This is the largest size appropriate for this type of construction.

Materials

Posts: A and B = 4 x 4 (3½ x 3½")

Cut wood: C = 2 x 4 (1½ x 3½")

Decking wood: D and E = 2 x 6 (1½ x 5½")

French wood screws
Wood screws

Instructions

1. Screw parts A and B together with French wood screws.

2. Roll the caisson into place and fill with stones. If the bottom leans, wedge under it with some small stones so that the stone caisson is level.

3. Screw boards C to the caisson; the two in the middle should be diagonally screwed.

4. Screw boards C together, securing the gangway to the center boards on the caisson.

5. Join the decking E to the stone caisson and the gangway with screws.

6. Firmly screw in rails D if you want a railing on one side. The top one should be approx. 36" above the pier decking.

Rules & regulations

Do I need a building permit?

You will need a building permit if you are constructing something new, or adding to or changing a building's use. A building permit is also necessary in many cases for building, for example, a privacy fence or an outer room. Check with your local authorities for the building codes, permit requirements in your neighborhood, and how to apply for a permit. Regulations on construction materials, methods, setbacks, and inspections vary from community to community. Often these regulations are posted online, but it is always best to speak face-to-face with someone who is familiar with them and can explain them to you. Do this early in the process to avoid any unpleasant surprises and unnecessary costs after the work is begun.

Normally a privacy fence has tightly-spaced boards that prevent visual intrusion, while a picket fence consists of stiles or boards spaced in a way that allows one to see in.

Some regulations apply at street crossings and crossways between street and bicycle paths, so that sight and, therefore, traffic safety will be not be impeded.

Always consider contacting the building regulators to find out what rules apply in your municipality.

Terraces and wood decks

The rules vary among municipalities and, therefore, you should always contact the building permit office in your town to be certain of what rules apply.

Finally

For areas outside detailed planning zones, certain regulations may apply. Contact the building permit office in your municipality so that they can provide you with information on which rules apply.

Finally, it is always a good idea to inform your neighbors about your plans. Being good neighbors avoids future conflicts and, in some cases, lawsuits. If they have legitimate concerns about what you are doing, address them in your plans.

Foundations

If you want to build a picket fence, a privacy fence, or another type of wood structure in your yard, it is important to begin with a good foundation. In this section, we present some examples of different ways to lay the foundation. Keep in mind that it is better to lay a stable foundation than something easier, because, after a few years, the fence will lean.

So that the ground won't create any problems for your yard structure, you should lay the foundation for a picket fence at least 18" deep, and for a privacy fence and other freestanding structures at least 24" deep. If you want to be completely on the safe side, you should go down to the frost-free depth. Ask the building authorities in your municipality for their recommendations.

When you dig the holes, all of the topsoil should be removed. If you have clay soil, you should remove a little more, going down further than the foundation depths given above, and fill up the hole with well-packed gravel.

Prepared plinths
This method of laying a foundation is suitable for shorter picket fences and other simple structures that won't be subject to high winds or other adverse conditions. If this method is used for a privacy fence, the fence must be reinforced against the wind. Otherwise, you can expect that eventually the privacy fence will lean.

Instructions
The plinths should be at least 24" tall. Dig a hole 8" deeper than the height of the plinth. Fill it with gravel or stone up to the level where the plinth will stand. Pack it well. Set the plinth in and adjust it carefully. Fix it into place with stones and gravel and, if possible, some coarse cement around the lower part of the plinth.

Metal post spike foundations
Metal post spike foundations are suitable only for shorter picket fences and simple structures. The foundation consists of a post box that is fastened to a pointed stake.

Instructions
Hammer the post spike into the ground with a sledge hammer. Place a wood block on the post box to protect it from the sledge hammer. When the foundation spike has been completely sunk, attach the fence post to the post box.

Bear in mind
• If you hit bedrock when hammering in a foundation, stop.
• It not possible to straighten the foundation afterwards.

A metal post spike foundation, at right, and a prepared plinth, below.

8" compacted gravel or stone.

Poured plinths

This is the best way to lay a foundation. The method is suitable for privacy fences up to 6' high and other structures where stronger environmental conditions must be taken into consideration, for example, a carport, pergola, and gazebos. If the construction will be subject to high winds, you should reinforce it in a suitable way so that it won't be damaged.

Instructions
Dig a hole about 40" deep or down to the frost-free depth. Pour an approximately 8" thick base plate of coarse cement in the bottom of the hole. Press 2 reinforcing rods into the center of the base plate before the concrete sets. When the base has set, place a casting form of cardboard (6–8" diameter) above the base. Fill the hole with soil around the cardboard tube. Fill the tube with coarse concrete and insert two post fasteners, ¼ x 1¾". These will stick up to varying heights above the concrete surface depending on the type of fastener used (see below). Straighten and hold them in place with a wood block until the concrete has set. You can use a post box instead of the post fasteners if the plinths will be used, for example, for a wood deck. Instead of the cardboard tube, you can use a concrete tube as the form.

Posts in the ground

This method of laying a foundation is suitable for shorter picket fences and other simple structures that will not be affected by strong winds or other elements. In this case you must use posts of pressure-treated wood.

Instructions
Dig a hole about 16" deep. Set the post in the hole and support it with stones and gravel in the bottom of the hole. Fill in with coarse concrete. Straighten and support the post before the concrete sets.

Bear in mind
• It is difficult to change the posts.
• It is even more difficult to adjust the posts.
• Make the hole deeper if the ground is clay or another frost heaving material.
• Even pressure-treated wood can gradually rot, particularly at the ground level.

Foundations into rock

One choice for laying a foundation into rock is a post box with a stud. A better alternative is to use a doubled rock stud fastener.

Instructions
Bore two holes for each post. Attach the rock stud fasteners by, for example, securing them with

The length of the post and height of the plinth is determined by what the plinth will be used for.

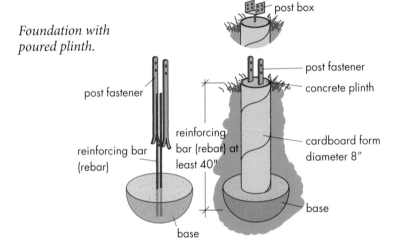

Foundation with poured plinth.

post box

post fastener

reinforcing bar (rebar)

post fastener

reinforcing bar (rebar) at least 40"

reinforcing bar (rebar)

concrete plinth

cardboard form diameter 8"

base

base

base

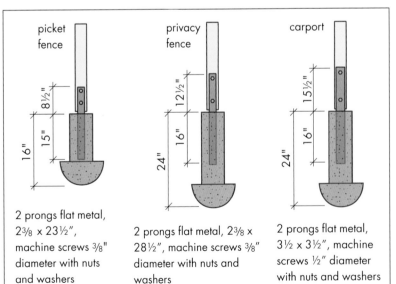

picket fence

8½"

15"

16"

2 prongs flat metal, 2⅜ x 23½", machine screws ⅜" diameter with nuts and washers

privacy fence

12½"

16"

24"

2 prongs flat metal, 2⅜ x 28½", machine screws ⅜" diameter with nuts and washers

carport

15½"

16"

24"

2 prongs flat metal, 3½ x 3½", machine screws ½" diameter with nuts and washers

expanding grout. The fastener has one round prong and a flat prong. The length of the flat metal piece depends on what you are fastening to the stud. For a picket fence, the flat prong could be 8" long or, for a privacy fence, 15".

Here's how to calculate the correct height of the plinths
When you are setting several plinths, for example, for a privacy fence or a carport, it is important that all the plinths are the right height. First set the plinth to the correct height according to the ground height. If you don't have access to a leveling instrument, use a square rule or a straight board and a level to align the next plinth. If the ground slopes and you have to set the plinths in stepwise, work the same way, taking the stepping down into consideration.

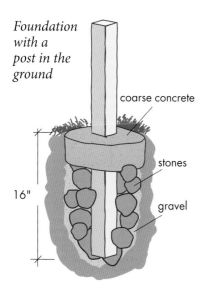

Foundation with a post in the ground

coarse concrete

stones

gravel

16"

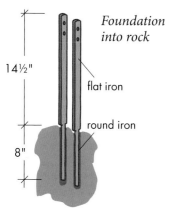

Foundation into rock

14½"

flat iron

round iron

8"

Common types of wood & their characteristics

Wood is one of the more proven building materials and, when untreated, is recyclable and thus suitable from an environmental standpoint. Pressure-treated wood is the exception and should be used as infrequently as possible.

The most common types of wood
In addition to native soft woods, like pine and spruce, some types of wood have been imported for exterior wood construction.

Spruce is a common conifer and is found in over 50 varieties. The tree has a straight trunk and grows to between 164 and 230 feet high. The crown is cone-shaped. The branches are more extensive than on a Scotch pine, so there are more twigs on a spruce. The twigs also fall away more easily when the wood dries. The wood is yellow-white, somewhat lighter than pine, and the surface wood has the same color as the core. Spruce is a soft type of wood, somewhat softer than pine. Its water absorption is lower than pine and, for that reason, spruce is considered more suitable for exterior panels. Spruce wood is less rot resistant than pine, which also makes it more difficult to deep treat it against rot.

Spruce is the most common type of wood used for building, particularly for most types of dimensional lumber and beams. It is also used for some types of carpentry, for example, paneling.

Pine is a conifer; it is also called fir. It is the most important type of tree within the building and carpentry trades, but also is important as an export. Pine grows over the entire northern half of the globe and can be found in over 90 varieties— everything from creeping to tall, straight trees 246–263' high. The pine is normally 66–98' high and is not one of the most quickly growing trees. For that reason, in the past few decades, it has been replaced, to some extent, by spruce in new tree plantings. The wood has a yellow-white color that changes over time. Splint wood (the surface wood) yellows, and the core wood (the innermost wood) becomes a darker red-brown when exposed to light. Pine contains more resin than spruce and is more rot resistant. The core wood contains materials that resist mold fungi. Pine wood is soft and usually has noticeably fewer twigs than spruce.

Pine is used primarily for all types of carpentry, furnishing, floors, and interior panelings, but also for building and pressure-treated wood.

Siberian Larch is a conifer that grows in the central areas of Siberia. It grows extremely slowly in the harsh climate, forming tight annual rings with a great deal of resin and oil in the tree. This gives the wood a natural resistance to rot. Additionally, the tree does not contain any environmental poisons and thus is more environmentally friendly than alternative pressure-treated woods. The wood is very hard compared with other conifers and the wood also has a larger amount of core wood than pine. The price is, of course, somewhat higher. The wood becomes silver grey as it ages if it is not treated. If you want to maintain the golden brown color you must treat the wood with oil.

Exterior uses for Siberian larch include profile-cut cladding, terraces, garden furniture, picket fences, and play equipment; interior uses include flooring and ceiling cladding.

FSC-forestry certification
FSC (the Forest Stewardship Council) is the first and only international certification system for the forestry and wood industries. The registered FSC trademark is an international guarantee of regulated forestry governed by environmental, social, and economic perspectives.

ITTO-rules
ITTO (the International Tropical Timber Organization) is an independent organization that works to preserve and maintain the tropical rain forests' resources. The 59 members represent approximately 80 percent of the world's rain forests and about 90 percent of the global sales of rainforest timber.

Bang Kirai is sometimes called bankirai, or simply kirai, but it is all the same product. Bang Kirai originated in Indonesia. It is a hard, weather-resistant wood similar to teak. The wood is oily and can be used untreated; it becomes silvery gray as it ages. To maintain the brown color, you must treat the surface with oil.

Bang Kirai is used most of all for exterior decking wood and it has a smooth and a corrugated side. The ridged side is the so called A-side, but the board can be reversed. Bang Kirai grows in forests managed according to ITTO-rules (see the box above).

Massaranduba originated in South America and is FSC-certified (see box above). This type of wood is sometimes called Brazilian redwood. It is a hardwood that is extremely durable. Massaranduba is primarily used for decking, in piers, and as pool decking because it is both fresh and salt water resistant and is extremely rot-resistant, even without being saturated by pressure-treating materials.

The lumber is sold with a smooth and a ridged side. It doesn't need to be treated on the surface, but if you want to maintain the warm red brown tone, it should be oiled.

Cumaru, or cumaro, is sometimes called Brazilian teak. This FSC-certified (see box) wood is very hard and weather resistant. Cumaru is completely maintenance free but, if it isn't treated, it ages and, over time, becomes silver gray.

Decking lumber is sold with a smooth side (the underside) and a ridged side (the top side).

Grading
Spruce and pine are graded according to SS-EN 1611-1 in the qualities G4-0, G4-1, G4-2, G4-3, and G4-4. The old grading symbols were O/S III (G4-0), O/S IV (G4-1), 5th (G4-2), discarded (G4-3) and ruined (G4-4).

The different grading classes and wood types are used as follows:

For building wood,
for example boards and sills:
    G4-2—G4-3, pine or spruce
For construction wood:
    G4-0—G4-2, pine or spruce
For unfinished
tongue-and-groove:
    G4-2—G4-3, pine or spruce
For form wood and packaging:
    G4-3, pine or spruce
For exterior paneling:
    G4-0—G4-1, spruce
For interior paneling:
    ≤G4-0—G4-2,
    pine or spruce

bang kirai

massaranduba

cumaru

For interior woodwork:
≤G4-0—G4-1, pine
For wood flooring:
≤G4-0—G4-2,
spruce or pine
For picket and privacy fences
G4-0—G4-2, spruce or pine
For rails:
≤G4-0—G4-1, pine

For the lowest lumber grading category, G4-4, there is no particular use. It is not used for any form of building or carpentry work.

For support constructions, such as roof trusses, construction lumber is used which is sorted into grades by wood strength: C30/K30, C24/K24, C18/K18 and C14/K12, where C24/K24 and C18/K18 are standard. Construction lumber is graded following set rules.

You can really recognize the lovely scent of fresh cut wood.

Definitions and terms

Cut or rough-sawn wood has all
 sides cut.
*Dimensional or Dimensioned
 planed wood* (also called
 planed wood) is planed to
 a specific dimension and is
 replacing cut wood more
 and more.
Unfinished planed wood is
 planed on at least two sides,
 most often three, with the
 fourth side cut.
S4S planed wood is planed on
 all four sides.
Tongue-and-groove has a tongue
 on one edge and a groove on
 the other for joining.

	Dimensions in inches (planed/cut)
Laths/battens	from ⅜ x 1" up to 1½ x 2"
Boards	from ⅜ x 3" up to 1⅜ x 8⅞"
Planks	from 1⅜ x 5⅞" up to 3¾ x 8⅞"
Lumber	from 1⅜ x 3" up to 1¾ x 8⅞"
Beams/rafters	from 2¾ x 3" up to 7⅞ x 8⅞"

The names and definitions can vary between lumber mills and building suppliers.

Handling wood correctly

Wood can be stored outdoors if it is protected from rain and sun. If it is to be used inside the house, it should be stored indoors at a low, even temperature. The wood should be stacked with spacing between the layers and held firm with a pressure band, so that it doesn't warp as it dries. You'll get the best results if you build with dry wood.

Glulam (glued laminated timber)

For longer spans of beams and roofing beams, glulam is recommended. Glulam is timber for beams and columns where several boards have been glued together with the grain lengthwise.

Pressure-treated wood

For most outdoor projects where the wood is affected by moisture or risks of insect attacks, the use of pressure-treated wood is recommended. It offers good protection against "wood-attacking organisms" (rot) and insects. However, don't use pressure-treated wood unless you have to, because it is environmentally damaging.

Various types of pressure treatments

Water-soluble solutions (salt treatment solutions) are the most common type, and the wood is recognizable by its green color. The wood is treated with a water-soluble solution that contains, for example, copper compounds. The wood's own characteristics do not change with this type of treatment, so the wood performs like untreated wood.

Oil-soluble solutions are used only for joinery work and are not dealt with in this book.

Creosote is produced from charcoal and used only on wood for posts, railroad ties, and wood exposed to a lot of moisture. This lumber should not be used in yards.

Wood rot-proofing grades

The wood rot-proofing grade **UC3A** is used for exterior woodwork such as doors and windows.

The wood rot-proofing grade **UC3B** is used for lumber exposed to weather and wind but is not in direct contact with water or the ground. It is used for structures where, from the perspective of safety, the bearing capacity and the possibility of easily changing out wood parts are not significant factors.

The wood rot-proofing grade **UC4B** is used for lumber exposed to fresh water or the ground and in constructions where bearing capacity is of significance from the safety perspective and where it can be difficult to inspect or change out the wood.

The wood rot-proofing grade **UC5, A, B, & C**, with a blue mark, is intended for lumber exposed to salt seawater, water, or used directly in the ground and whenever there is a necessity for extra durability and resistance.

Finishing

Lumber that has been pressure-treated with water-soluble solutions can be finished the same way as untreated wood. It does not need additional finishing from an aesthetic point of view. To avoid cracks, for example, in terrace flooring and unpainted garden furniture and other outdoor structures, you should treat the wood with wood oil now and then. See "Wood Finishing," on page 118 for more information.

A well-oiled, pressure-treated decking effectively sheds water and will look good for many years.

Panels

For many years, panels have been an important part of all building construction. Panels have developed over the years and the time is past when panels in a construction usually consisted of three tex sheets on the inside of walls. Today, plasterboard, MDF sheets, and plywood are the most used. The most common sheets for exterior use are the following:

Plywood
Plywood consists of veneers glued together with each new layer glued with the grain perpendicular to the previous layer. The material used in this type of panel is usually spruce or pine. Plywood is a flexible but strong material that can be bent. The planned use determines the type of plywood to choose. Panels for exterior use need a specific kind of glue. The two types that currently are favored for exterior use are construction plywood and form plywood.

Construction plywood is used for support constructions and is durability graded P30. The panels can be used in all environments, irrespective of humidity. It is manufactured with spruce or pine.

Thickness: ¼–1"
Size: 4 x 8'

Form plywood is used for constructing casting forms and is treated for water resistance. For that reason, it can also be suitable for some exterior woodwork. It is usually browner in color than other types of plywood and the sheets are covered by a film for water resistance. The edges are also sealed and, when the panels have been cut, the edges should be resealed. The surface veneer is usually birch, while the interior veneers are most often conifer.

Thickness: ⅜–1⅛"
Size: 2 x 8', 4 x 4', 4 x 8'

OSB
OSB (Oriented Strand Board) is a newer variation of plywood that is actually something between plywood and particle board. It is a very durable panel and consists of particles that have been glued together. When coated with a protective surface it can be used for exterior constructions. This type of panel is still a rather expensive choice.

Thickness: varies depending on the manufacturer; the most common is ½".
Size: varies depending on the manufacturer; the most common is approximately 4 x 8'.

MDF
MDF (Medium Density Fiberboard) is a type of panel manufactured from small bits of wood particles that are baked together with a glue to form a cake. The small particles produce a harder panel with a finer surface than, for example, particle board, but it is also heavier. The sheets hold their shape well and are easy to work with. The most common MDF panels are used primarily for interior woodwork, but now there are also MDF panels with a high moisture resistance, making it suitable for exterior use.

Thickness: ⅛–¾"
Size: from ⅜" thickness and up; panels are manufactured in the dimensions 4 x 8'.

From the bottom up:
Construction plywood
Form plywood
OSB panel
MDF panel

111

Sizing

Sizing a wood structure is not something you should approach as an amateur. We'll show you some ready solutions with appropriate dimensions for the projects in this book. If you are thinking about other options than those shown here, we recommend that you consult a contractor who can help you avoid problems in the future. In some cases, the building codes in a community require that a construction be calculated following regulations.

In order to understand the process, it's important to know a few basics:

1. A board on edge is preferable to a square board. Why?
Flexural rigidity, that is, how much the board bends when stressed, increases by 8 times if the height is doubled. If the width is doubled, the flexibility only doubles.
   Flexural strength, how much the board can tolerate, increases by 4 times when the height is doubled but only doubles when the width is doubled.

2. A board on edge is preferable to a board lying flat. Why?
If we consider that the boards have the same stress, a board on edge has more than 200 percent better flexural rigidity than a board lying flat. In regards to flexural strength, the standing board has 50 percent more bending resistance than the flat board.

3. It is better to choose a board on edge with a somewhat smaller center distance than a square board with a longer center distance. Why?
The wood's own weight increases with a square board without the rigidty increasing noticeably. In addition, it is better to have a smaller distance between the boards when you are choosing, for example, decking. Otherwise, the decking boards will bend more.

4. Decking boards are not joined on every board. Why?
Bending (bending down) is much greater than if one allows the flooring stress to go over several boards. Therefore it is also better with a smaller center distance between the beams, as in point 3 above.

5. Two adjoining pieces of decking are not joined on the same joist. Why?
Bending (bending downwards) is greater if you let the joins extend; there should be at least two boards between two joins on the same joist.

If you choose other measurements for your terrace or carport than those we show in our projects, you can also find sizing help in the booklet online or in textbooks. You'll find ample tables for terraces and exterior roofing as well as much more information about wood products.

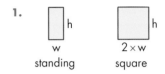

1.

standing   square

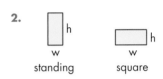

2.

standing   square

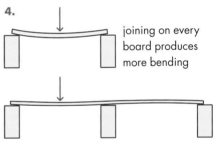

3.

right

standing, less

wrong

square, larger

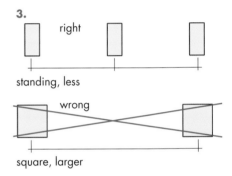

4.

joining on every board produces more bending

joining on every other board or every third board produces less bending.

5.

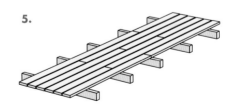

Joining wood

Whenever you work with wood, you will need to join different pieces of wood. There are quite a few ways to do this: nail, screw, bolt, or with fittings that, in turn, are nailed or screwed. Sometimes you need to finish the join with glue. For outdoor constructions, it is important to use the right type of glue.

Nailing
This is the easiest way to join and has been used for a long time. For a durable join, nailing is often combined with gluing.

• Choose a nail with a length about 2.5 times the thickness of what will be connected if you are joining wood to wood.
• Don't nail too close to the end of the wood or on the edge because the wood can split.
• If you are going to spackle and paint the surface, for example, on a rail, choose brads. Even with hidden nailing, for example, when you join a panel by nailing into tongue-and-groove, use brads.
• For exterior constructions, use galvanized or rustproof nails.

There are many kinds of nails. We've shown some of the most common.

Wire nails. Ridged shaft and flat head. Used for interior construction and joinery to join boards, roof trusses, etc.

Brads. Ridged shaft and conical head. Used for hidden nailing when the head will be countersunk or if you are spackling and painting the surface.

Roofing nails: Round shaft and flat, large head. Used for nailing in roofing felt and boards on wood underlay.

Cut nails. Round, cut shaft and flat, countersunk head. Used for nailing plaster board to wood boards.

Threaded nails. Round, threaded shaft and flat or low rounded head. Used wherever there is a greater need for long-term strength.

Bracket nails. Round, threaded shaft and softly rounded head. Used for nailing sheet metal to wood. It sometimes includes a grommet.

Nail anchors. Round, threaded shaft and flat, countersunk head. Used together with building fittings.

Screws

Joining with screws has become much more common. The development of screws for various purposes has been rapid, and more and more special screws mean that their use has spread. The price of tools has dropped and, today, everybody has an electric screwdriver.

• Choose a screw length two times the thickness of what you will screw together.

The appearance of screws varies depending on the purpose and the manufacturer. Here are a few general types and options. Talk with your building or lumber supplier for help in choosing the right screw for your purpose.

Finishing

The most common screws for exterior use are galvanized, finished with Sandbond-Z or are rustproof.

Head

The top photo below shows a number of common heads for wood screws (1–5).
The most common heads are:
• flat, countersunk heads that produce a countersunk profile in wood, particle board, plywood, and wood fiber panels. It must be countersunk beforehand.
• round heads for a visible screw.
• round countersunk heads for a visible and partially countersunk head.

• trumpet heads on plaster screws.
• flat, countersunk heads with milled ribs on the underside. The ribs mill a flat surface without needing to be countersunk beforehand.

The development of screw drivers with bits has also influenced the development of screw heads, so that, today, you can also find heads for special purposes. Furthermore, there are a number of screw heads for various special screws.

Screw drive types

There are many varieties of drive types on screws; see the photos at right below (11–15). Make sure that you choose the correct bit for the screw you are using, considering both type and size; otherwise the drive can easily be ruined. The straight drive is the one with the least adjustments for bits and screw drivers.

Square or hexagonal drives are also available on some products.

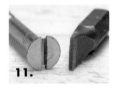

1. Flat, countersunk head
2. Round head
3. Round, countersunk head
4. Trumpet head
5. Flat, countersunk head with milled ribs
6. Screw with milled grooves at the point
7. Screw with bore point
8. Self-cutting point
9. Screw with reverse threading
10. Screw with milled threading
11. Straight drive
12. Philips head (Ph)
13. Pozidriv (Pz)
14. Torx (T)
15. Lox

Different points
The center photo to the left on the previous page shows three different point styles (6–8):
• threaded points are the most common
• bore points means that the screw can bore into the material without counterboring
• milled tracks at the point reduce the risk for splintering, but you do need to counterbore

Talk with your building or lumber supplier for recommendations on the type of screws to use for your purposes.

Threading
Heavy threads, steeply wound, are used for wood. These screws will go into the wood fast.

Low threads, closely wound, are used for hard, tropical wood types.

High-low threading is suitable for plaster boards.

There are even other types of threads for screwing into concrete, brick, cinder blocks, etc.

Screws with reverse threading (9) have threads that wind to the left on the part of the shaft just below the head. These tighten into the work more easily.

Screws with milled threading (10) change the steepness of the winding between the normal threading and the smooth part of the screw, and mill away the threads created in the wood when the first part of the screw is screwed in. This means that the resistance diminishes, and the smooth, upper part of the screw glides more easily into the hole when you tighten the pieces together.

Bolts

Another way to join wood is to bolt it. There are several types of bolts used for building and woodworking. For exterior construction, always use galvanized bolts. Here are some examples:

Hex bolts
This is a common type of bolt that can be partially or completely threaded. The most common sizes are M6, M8, M10, and M12. They come in various lengths from 1⅜" and longer. Hexagonal bolts are used when bolting completely through along with washers, round or square; nuts are the best alternative.

Considerations
• use washers so that the bolts and nuts are not in direct contact with the wood
• if you choose a partially threaded bolt, make sure that the unthreaded section is inside the construction

Carriage bolts
Carriage bolts are used as through bolts. They have a round head that does not stick up very much from the surface of the wood. A square section beneath the head means that the bolt won't turn when the nut is tightened. The most common sizes are M6, M8, M10, and M12. Carriage bolts are available in lengths 1" and longer. Don't forget to use a washer with a carriage bolt even at the head so that the bolt doesn't tighten in the wood.

French wood screws
This type of bolt is between a screw and a bolt. Use them when you cannot use a through bolt but need a strong screw. The most common sizes are ⅛", ¼", ⅜", and ½" in lengths

1. Hex or hexagonal bolt
2. Carriage bolt
3. French wood screw
4. Nuts and washers

1" and longer. Don't forget to counterbore; otherwise you risk splintering. Use a washer so you can press the screw hard without forcing it into the wood.

Nuts and washers
Nuts come in many varieties and sizes. Both round and square washers are available in many sizes.

Construction fasteners

Construction fasteners can be used for almost all wood joins. They are manufactured from galvanized steel plate in many varieties and sizes. Construction fasteners are made with one or more holes so they can be attached with screws or nails. The most common are those used with anchor screws or nail anchors. Usually they offer the best and most economical results because fewer screws or nails need to be used. How many nails/screws are necessary in each fastener varies from case to case, but three nails/screws per fastener is a good rule of thumb. You shouldn't fill in all the holes with nails/screws because that increases the risk of the wood splitting. Also remember not to nail or screw too near the ends of the lumber.

Here are some of the most common fittings:

Nail plate (1)
Used as a joint plate for connecting wood to, for example, roof trusses.

Joist hanger (2)
Used for connecting wood beams on the same plane.

Corner brackets (3)
Used to connect crossing beams, roof ridges or between beam and column connections. Can be used with or without reinforcement.

1. Nail plate
2. Joist hanger
3. Corner bracket
4. Roof ridge connector
5. Universal fitting
6. Fork anchor

1.

2.

3.

4.

5.

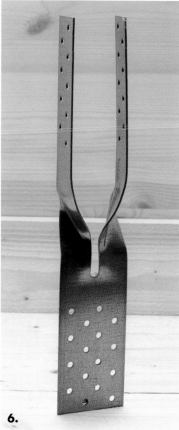

6.

Roof ridge connector (4)
Used for crossing connections, for example, when firmly anchoring roof trusses on the beam.

Universal fitting (5)
Used for cross connections, for example, for anchoring a roof ridge to an underlying beam that leans slightly.

Fork anchor (6)
Used to anchor roof trusses or beams to underlying wood construction.

Glue
The most common type of wood glue is a *1-component glue* based with PVAc (polyvinyl acetate). The glue is water soluble and is not diluted when used. There are glues for various purposes:

Wood glue, interior: Only for interior use. Apply at temperatures of 64 to 68ºF / +18 to + 20ºC.

Wood glue, winter: Only for interior use. Apply in temperatures down to 14ºF / -10 ºC.

Wood glue, exterior: Used when a moisture-resistant glue is needed, for example, outdoors. Apply at temperatures of 64 to 68ºF / +18 to + 20ºC.

There are also *2-component glues* based with PVAc. This type of glue is used when moisture resistance is needed and water resistance is high. The glue consists of a base and a hardener. It should be used at temperatures of 64ºF / +18ºC and higher.

There are also some special types of glue, including those with polyurethane as a binder, for gluing particular types of materials. Inquire about these at your building or paint supplier.

Work methods
(for both interior and exterior wood glue)
1. The pieces should be clean and fit each other well. The parts should have a temperature of approx. 64ºF /+18ºC and a maximum humidity level of 8–12 percent.

2. Apply the glue in even strokes on one or both surfaces. If the glue is applied to both surfaces, the adhesion will be stronger.

3. Set both parts together within 5 minutes, while the glue is still flowing.

4. Press the parts together and hold them under pressure for 5–15 minutes, until there is strong adhesion. The amount of compression time depends on a number of different factors and so can vary accordingly. You don't have to worry about this if you combine gluing with screwing or nailing.

Wood finishing

All exterior wood must be finished, partly to protect the wood from drying out and absorbing water, and partly to give the wood a nice appearance. If you don't finish the wood, the surface will become ugly, and there is also the risk that the wood will split and rot. After a while, untreated wood grays and it is not possible to paint such a surface. So, make sure that you treat the wood as soon as possible, if you want a good covering coat. Pigment paints can be used to advantage if the wood has been exposed to weather and wind for a while.

Humidity
Test the amount of humidity in the wood you are going to paint. The humidity level should not rise above 16%; otherwise, there is the risk of bubbles forming in the paint. Humidity can be measured with a hygrometer. Wait a while if the humidity is too high and test again when the wood has dried somewhat.

Season and weather
You should do outdoor painting between May and September. The weather should be warm and dry, but you should avoid painting in strong, direct sunlight. The appropriate temperature for painting varies for different types of paint. Linseed oil-based paint dries slowly if the temperature is below 64°F / 18°C, and water-borne paints should not be used if the temperature is below 45°F / 7°C.

Pressure-treated wood
Pressure-treated wood with water-soluble impregnation can be finished the same way as untreated wood. It doesn't need to be finished any further for aesthetic reasons either. To avoid cracks in, for example, terrace flooring, garden furniture, or other constructions that people come into direct contact with, the wood should be treated with wood oil. Don't forget to allow the same amount of time between repeat coats. Pressure-treated wood that is oiled becomes darker with each treatment.

Wood with other types of penetrating treatments might not need to be finished, or they might need special treatment. Ask at the paint shop about finishing woods penetrated with these solutions.

Paint systems
There are a number of different paint "systems" to use when finishing wood. Special covering paints require that the work be carried out with those products in the application sequence that the manufacturer recommends.

Maintenance
Generally, covering paints should be renewed every ten years, for example, on a wood façade. Stains should be renewed more often. Pigment paints can last many years without maintenance.

Maintenance painting
If a wood surface needs to be repainted, you should begin by washing the wood with some type of paint cleaner. If algae have built up on the surface of the paint, use algae and mold-resistant cleaner. Rinse off and let dry well. If the surface was cover painted you may need to scrape off any loose paint before you repaint. If you have a clean wood surface, you should treat it as if painting it for the first time; otherwise, it works well enough to apply a coat of the same type of paint as used on the wood before. Don't mix paint types; use the paint system you used previously. If you want to change, you should ask your paint dealer about the options.

Pigment paint
Pigment paint, for example, Swedish Falu red, is a matte paint that is produced from wheat or rye meal with boiled linseed oil as the binder. Pigment paint should not be used on planed wood or wood previously treated with another type of paint. The paint is moisture permeable but has a certain amount of water resistance during the first few years. The wood can "breathe" through pigment paint.

Suitable purposes: façades, picket and privacy fences.

Initial painting: coat twice with pigment paint.

Linseed oil paint
Linseed oil-based paint contains linseed oil as the binder. The paint also contains pigment and other chemicals. After painting, the surface remains shiny for the first few years but becomes flat over time. This facilitates maintenance.

118

Suitable purposes: façades, picket and privacy fences, gates and rails.

Initial painting: prime with linseed oil diluted with 8 oz. ligroin per quart of paint for better penetration. Let the paint dry at least one day and then add another coat without diluting the linseed oil paint. For exposed surfaces, an intermediate coat with a little less dilution is recommended. Bear in mind that drying times will be longer.

Alkyd oil-based paint
Alkyd oil-based paint was developed from linseed oil paint and, in principle, has better qualities. The paint was previously dissolved in ligroin but now there are even water-borne forms. The paint is appropriate for places that are particularly exposed to moisture and where there is a great need for mechanical tolerance. The drying time is longer than for acrylic paint. Alkyd paint produces a shinier surface than acrylic paints (see below).

Suitable purposes: façades, picket and privacy fences, gates and rails.

Initial painting: wood ends, joins, and other exposed areas or whole surfaces. When you want to be extra careful and create a deeply penetrating moisture protection, coat with oil painting primer. Next, cover the surface with a pigmented primer to provide a good adhesive surface for alkyd paints. The primer seals and shields further against moisture. Afterwards, apply two coats of alkyd paint.

Acrylic paint
Acrylic paint is an alternative for alkyd paint when moisture exposure is normal. The paint is water-borne and must be used in combination with oil painting primer and primer paint.

Suitable purposes: façades, picket and privacy fences, gates and rails.

Initial painting: Coat once with oil painting primer over the entire surface to create a deep penetrating shield against moisture. Next, apply a coat of pigmented primer to provide an adhesive surface for acrylic paint. The primer also further seals against moisture. Finish with two coats of acrylic paint.

Covering stain
Covering stain is between stain and covering paint. The surface is covered but the wood structure holds up better than painting with a covering paint.

Suitable purposes: façades, picket and privacy fences, gates and rails.

Initial painting: Coat once with an oil painting primer and twice with covering stain. Let the oil and stain dry between coats. If the façade really absorbs the oil primer on the first coat, you can apply a coat of primer, before applying the finishing paint.

Stain
Stain contains a lower amount of pigment than regular paint. This means that the wood structure is visible through the paint. Stains need more maintenance than other paints, but the maintenance is easy to carry out. After washing you normally need only one coat with a colorless or weak pigmented stain.

Suitable purposes: façades, picket and privacy fences, exterior stairs and outdoor flooring.

Initial painting: Coat once with colorless stain and then twice with stain in one color. The paint deepens and penetrates less if you apply two coats. Let the stain dry between coats.

Wood protection oil
There are both solvent-borne and water-borne alkyd oils. Wood oil resists splitting, discoloring, and water penetration. Pressure-treated wood should not be treated sooner than one year.

Suitable purposes: exterior stairs, outdoor flooring, piers and garden furniture.

Initial painting: coat well with oil using a brush or rag until the surface is saturated. Leave for half an hour. Wipe off any extra oil with a lint-free rag or cotton waste.

Small buildings

A shed can be used, in principle, for anything, such as storage, a sauna, a guest cottage, or a wood shed.

Planning

Look around your lot. What do you need? What is it possible to build? Do you want to hide the shed or let it be part of the yard as a whole?

Further considerations

• Talk with your neighbors. Even if you build more than far enough from the property line and don't need their consent, be a good neighbor and discuss what your plans are before you build.

• It is always best to contact the building permits office to see what pertains to your situation.

• Fit the shed to the surroundings. It is important that, even if it is small, it fits in with all the other buildings in terms of style and color. There are certainly no special rules regarding color and design but, if you don't take those aspects into consideration, even a small shed will negatively affect the overall look of your house and yard.

• Decide what type of foundation the shed will have. This book discusses foundations with plinths , the most common base for simple sheds (see the chapter "Foundations" on page 105). Otherwise, follow the building instructions for the particular project.

We hope you'll be inspired by the projects on the following pages.

Bicycle shed

This bicycle shed, which is 23 square feet and somewhat hidden by the greenery in a corner of the garden, has room for the family's five bicycles, bicycles that we previously stumbled over just outside the front door. So, after unlocking the bikes and letting the seats dry, we are on the way in the morning and the front yard is orderly.

Materials

The bicycle shed was constructed with oil-treated larch wood. Larch is a very water-resistant wood but, of course, it's also fine to build the shed with pressure-treated wood or unfinished wood that can be finished.

Posts, 4 x 4 (3½ x 3½"):
    3 pieces each 84" (A1)
    2 pieces each 79" (A2)

Joist, 2 x 4 (1½ x 3½"):
    2 pieces each 120" (B)

Roof supports, 2 x 6 (1½ x 5½")
    5 pieces each 120" (C)

Support battens, 1 x 2 (¾ x 1½")
    6 pieces each 124" (D)

Fascia boards, 1 x 6 (¾ x 5½")
    2 pieces each 120" (E
    1 piece 125½" (F)

Covering boards for the underside of the roof beams, 1 x 4 (¾ x 3½")
    3 pieces each 120" (G)

Frame for the door, 1 x 2 (¾ x 1½") (H)
    approx. 28'

Wall and door paneling, 1 x 3 (¾ x 2½")
    24 pieces each, 120¾" (I and M)
    1 piece 80½" (J)
    21 pieces each 40" (K)
    21 pieces each 55¼" (L)
    3 pieces each 96" (N)

Plinths: 5
Hexagonal bolts, nuts, and washers for the plinths
Wood screws
Hinges: 2
Corrugated plastic for the roof
Sheet metal cladding roof trim
Handles, locks for the door

Instructions

Here's a shed set in a corner of the yard with a high hedge around it. The hedge functions as a wall on two of the sides, while the other two sides are wood paneled. You can, of course cover all the walls with wood if you want. The shed doesn't have any gutters, so the rain water runs down in the hedge.

1. Bury the five plinths (see page 105).

2. Roughly cut the posts A1 & A2 and place them in the plinths. Check to be sure they are level and mark how they should be cut. Take the posts down, make notches (1½ x 3½") for the joists B and, finally, mount them to the plinths with hexagonal bolts, nuts, and washers. Throughout, carefully check with a level to make sure they are vertical.

3. Set in and screw the joists B firmly between the two posts on the long sides.

4. Set up the roof beams C and mark the cutting lines on the ends—they should extend out about 12" on both sides. Take them down and cut them. Place them all next to each other and mark the notches (¾ x 1½") for the support battens D. Set a circular saw to a ¾" depth and cut all the notches at the same time. Finish the cuts with a chisel.

5. Set up the roof beams C and screw them in.

6. Lay the support battens D in the notches and screw them in firmly.

7. Screw the fascia boards F securely to the roof beams C on the long sides which will be covered with wood paneling. Screw the wind boards E firmly into the support battens D and into fascia boards F.

8. Screw the covering boards G onto the underside of the parts that extend out from the roof beams, on the long side that will be covered with wood paneling.

9. Construct the frame H for the door and attach it to the door opening with hinges on one side and temporarily with a couple of screws on the other side.

10. Screw on the wall and door paneling I, K, L, M, and N. Note that the paneling on the door covers the corner post and that the paneling M on the wall extends out ¾" and thus covers the end wood on the door paneling boards. Also note that the top wall panel N on the short side needs to be fitted at the top to follow the roof line.

11. Mount an upright J centered on the inside of the long wall as a support for the wall paneling.

12. Remove the temporary fastening on the door. Choose the type of handle or lock you want and attach it.

13. Finish with a coat of oil for larch wood or pressure-treated wood. Paint or stain if you made the shed with untreated wood.

14. Attach the plastic roof and then the sheet metal cladding all around.

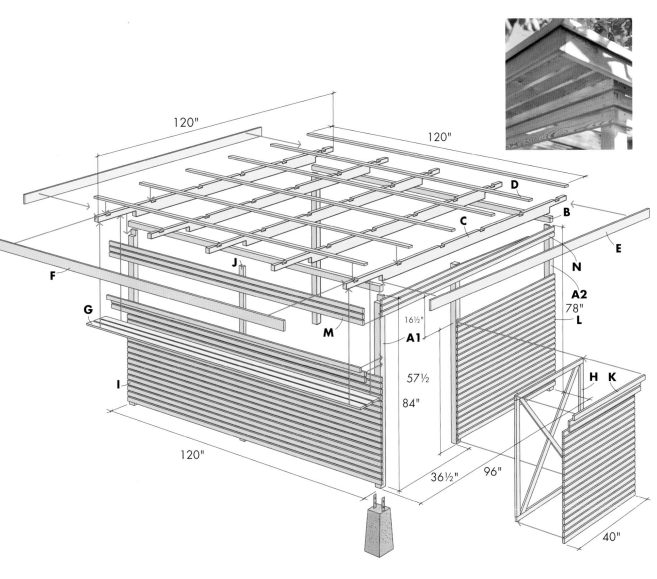

120"

120"

D

C

B

E

N

A2
78"
L

16½"

A1

J

M

F

G

I

120"

57½

84"

H K

36½" 96"

40"

Playhouse

Just imagine—your own little playhouse! Even children need
a place where they can be alone or together with friends—
without grown-ups disturbing them. This small red cottage with
white trim has made many children happy. It has already been
passed down through three generations, and, with a little
upkeep, will last for many more years.

Materials for the foundation
Sand or gravel
Light cinder blocks: 6

Materials for the playhouse
Pressure-treated 2 x 4 (1½ x 3½")
2 pieces each 108" (A1)
6 pieces each 59" (A2)
3 pieces each 28½" (A3)
2 pieces each 13½" (A4)

Unfinished tongue-and-groove, 1
x 4 (¾ x 3½"), approx.:
34 square feet (B)
80 square feet (H)

4 x 4 (3½" x 3½")
2 pieces each 60" (C1)
2 pieces each 30" (C2)

Decking, 1 x 4 (¾ x 3½")
approx. 13 square feet (D)

2 x 4 (1½ x 3½")
2 pieces each 78" (E1)
1 piece 55" (E1)
2 pieces each 15" (E1)
16 pieces each 53" (E2)
2 pieces each 78" (E3)
2 pieces each 55" (E3)
4 pieces each approx. 60" (E4)
4 pieces each approx. 24" (E5)
2 pieces each 18" (E6)
10 pieces each 52" (F)
2 pieces each 26½" (N)
2 pieces each 10¾" (N)

1 x 3 (¾ x 2½")
5 pieces each 8" (G1)
5 pieces each 30" (G2)
4 pieces each 52" (T)
2 pieces each 26½" (P)
2 pieces each 10¾" (P)
4 pieces each 16" (Q)
6 pieces each 26½" (R)

Dowels 1" diameter,
16 pieces each 21" (O)

Triangular rails, 2 x 2"
4 pieces each 52" (I)

2 x 2 (1½ x 1½")
6 pieces each 21½" (J)

Single tongue-and-groove,
1 x 4 (¾ x 3½"), approx.
115 square feet (K)

Exterior paneling boards, 1 x 4
(¾ x 3½"), approx. 20' (L)

Exterior paneling boards, 1 x 5
(¾ x 4½") approx. 53' (M)

Exterior fascia boards, 1 x 6 (¾ x
5½"), approx. 22' (S)

Windows: 2 (buy ready-made)
Roofing underlayment
Corner brackets: 8
French wood screws: 4
Wood screws
Nails
Roofing felt and asphalt adhesive
for 80 square feet
Roofing nails

Materials for the door
Plywood, ⅝"
2 pieces each 24 x 24"(U)
Bead board, 5/16 x 3⅛"
approx. 23' (V)
8 pieces ripped to 1" wide,
each 24" (X1)
4 pieces each 7" (X2)
4 pieces each 9" (X3)

1 x 3 (¾ x 3½")
2 pieces each 53¾" (Y1)
1 piece 26½" (Y2)
2 pieces each 53¾" (Z1)
1 piece 25" (Z2)

Glass, ⅛", 7 x 7"

Hinges: 4
Door handle
Sliding bolts: 2
Glue
Wood screws
Nails

This is an old playhouse but the building instructions given here are suitable for today's dimensional standards. The profile-cut decorative boards and turned fence rails are made from straight boards and dowels. If you are really ambitious, you can cut the profiles (see drawing) and turn the rails.

Instructions for the playhouse
1. Begin by removing all the topsoil where the playhouse will be situated. Pour in gravel or sand and compact it to at least 4" thick. Set out the cinderblocks and make sure that they are all at the same level.

2. Nail or screw the foundation frame A together. Note that there should be two A2 boards at the very front and that the outer one should be 1½" in from the end of A1. Set the frame on the cinder blocks, with underlayment between the frame and blocks. Measure the diagonals to ensure they are equal and make sure that the frame corners are all at a 90° angle. Also make sure that the frame is completely level.

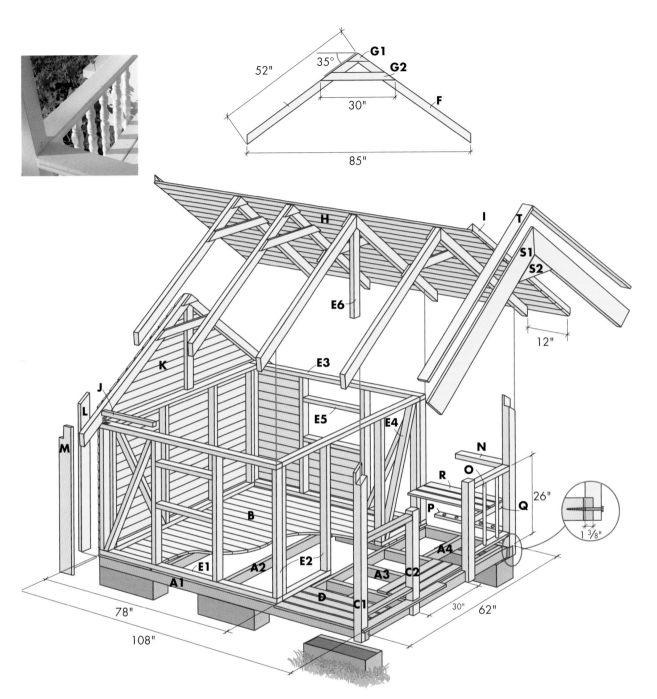

3. Nail the unfinished tongue-and-groove flooring B with the planed side up inside the cottage. Use brads and nail into the grooves to hide the nail heads.

4. Cut and attach the posts C2. Cut the posts C1 only on the lower edge and temporarily attach them.

5. Screw on the decking boards. Cut the notches for posts C.

6. Screw the sills E1 to the unfinished tongue-and-groove and foundation frame. Take the width of the door into consideration.

7. Attach uprights E2 by screwing them in diagonally or using the corner brackets. Take the width of the window into consideration.

8. Going in from the top, screw in the top piece of the frame E3 firmly. Use a level to make sure that the frame is squared and then mount the diagonals E4.

9. Frame in the window to accomodate the window you have chosen.

10. Screw the roof trusses together, beginning with one and then using it as a template.

Set up the trusses and screw them together firmly with corner brackets. Secure them with diagonal braces if necessary. Hold off joining the front roof truss for the time being. First, measure and mark where the posts C1 will be cut, take them down and cut the joint recesses. Attach the posts C1 with French wood screws and screw them firmly into the last roof truss.

11. Screw horizontal braces J between the roof trusses so that the outer edges align with the outer edges of the frame E; the exterior paneling will be attached to them.

12. Nail on the unfinished tongue-and-groove roof panels H, with the panels extending slightly more than 12" beyond the outer roof trusses. Cut them cleanly 12" from the end of the trusses when everything is in place. Firmly nail on the triangular rails G.

13. Lay the roofing felt on with roofing nails and asphalt glue (see instructions on the packaging).

14. Set the fascia boards S1 and S2 into place as well as the caps T.

15. Nail on the exterior paneling K.

16. Set in the window and door (see below); the frames should be aligned with the panels.

17. Screw the corner boards L onto the corners of the gable ends and then uprights M on the long sides and around the window and door.

18. Bore holes for the rods into boards N and P. Join N, P, and O and screw them firmly into place.

19. Screw on seat support boards Q and, finally, the seat boards R.

Instructions for the Door

1. Cut the hole for the glass in the upper door panel U. Draw a line centered on the panel, cut strips V (at a 45° angle), glue and nail them on with thin nails.

2. Screw on and glue the strips X1 around the door panels and X2 on the window hole. Set in the glass and screw on the batten X3, without glue, on the inside.

3. Glue and firmly screw parts Z into Y for the door frame and screw them securely into the door opening.

4. Attach the door panels with hinges and attach the door handle and sliding bolts.

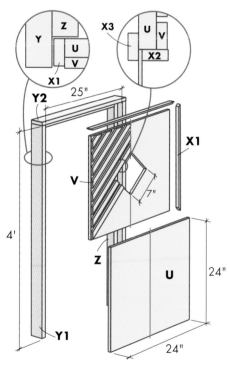

Firewood rack

It's very practical to have a little rack with firewood near the house. It protects the wood against direct rain at the same time as it lets the wood air properly so it stays "fresh" longer.

Materials
Lumber, 2 x 4 (1½ x 3½")¹
    2 pieces each 66" (A)
    6 pieces each 52" (C)
    4 pieces each approx. 58" (D)
    2 pieces each 48" (E)
    4 pieces each 60" (F)

Wood screws
Bricks: 9
Roof tiles: 18
Materials for the foundation
    (see page 106)

Instructions
1. Cut the two back uprights A (the legs) a bit longer than the finished measurements. Thoroughly oil the parts that will be sunk into the ground.

2. Dig the postholes for the two legs A (see "Setting posts in the ground," page 106). Make sure the posts are vertical and the correct distance from each other by temporarily nailing or clamping them with the crossbars.

3. Lay out the bricks B.

4. Cut the 6 floor boards C and set them into place.

5. Cut the remaining four legs D.

6. Counterbore and attach the legs to the floor boards with long screws.

7. Cut the joists E, which connect the legs, with a slight downward slope. Hold them with clamps. Measure carefully and use a level to make sure that all the legs and floor are squared and level. Even the bricks must be aligned correctly.

8. Counterbore and attach the joists to the legs with long screws.

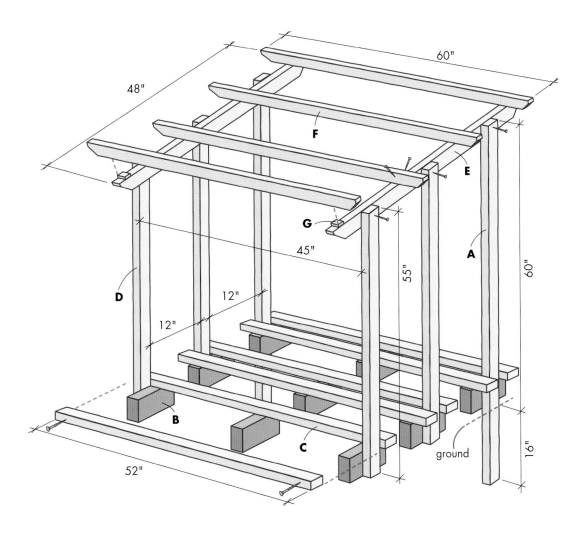

9. Cut the legs even with the top of the joists.

10. Cut the 4 roof beams F and lay them in place. Lay on the roof tiles to make sure that the beams are placed correctly. Attach blocks G (the same thickness as the roof tiles) underneath the front beam.

11. Set the roof tiles into place and fill the rack with wood.

Carefully chopped and stacked wood is lovely and makes such a homey feeling.

Shower stall

Slightly hidden and private amidst the pines and leafy trees but only a stone's throw from the house—a little shower stall. Here's a place where one can spend some quiet time under the tree tops, with the blue sky as the roof on a warm summer day. Or, what the owner of the shower has described as something particularly special, to go out and take a warm shower when it is pouring rain!

Materials

A poured foundation or 6 plinths (see page 105).

2 x 3 (1½ x 2½")'
    15 pieces each approx. 36" (A)
    2 pieces each 72"(B)
    4 pieces each approx. 48"(D)
    2 pieces each approx. 36" (F)
    1 piece approx. 48" (G)

1 x 3 (¾ x 2½")
    112 pieces, each 72" (C)

Cut wood, 1 x 4 (¾ x 3½")
    6 pieces just over 38"(E)

Mounts: 6
Nail plates
Anchor screws
Wood screws
Wood oil
Shower set with mixer

Lake stones have been added on the cast plate. This makes the stall's floor beautiful to look at as well as soft and comfortable to stand on.

Instructions

The shower stall shown here has a hexagonal poured concrete slab, but you can use six plinths and set stones in the ground instead.

The frame has corner posts only at the door, so the covering boards in the corners must be screwed in firmly when the frame is constructed because they hold the stall together.

1. Pour a hexagonal concrete slab, with each side 39" long. Set in the mounts for the boards and don't forget the drain.

A simpler alternative is to bury 6 plinths (see page 105) and setting stones in the ground.

2. Cut 15 boards A with a 30° angle at the ends. Calculate the length based on how far they will be set inside the edge of the base. To make the horizontal frames, attach the boards in groups of five with small nail plates and anchor screws.

3. Connect the lower horizontal frame to the set-in mounts or plinths. If the distance between the connectors on the plinths is too great for your boards, remove one connector with an angle grinder and then attach the boards with French wood screws to the remaining fasteners.

4. Mount posts B at the door and two wall boards C on the outside in the opposite corner. Make sure that there is at least an inch space between the slab and the posts and wall boards.

5. Mount the two remaining horizontal frames. Make sure that they are level and that the distance between the three frames is the same.

6. Screw on the wall boards in the two remaining corners.

7. Cut and attach the diagonal braces D with screws into the frame following the illustration.

8. Cut all the wall boards and screw them into the frames. There should be ten on each outside wall and nine on each inside. Space them so that the distance between them on each of the sides is even.

Consider cutting the boards angled upwards so that the covering boards E on the top can slope. The boards should be cut at an angle on the bottom for water runoff. Note that the inner boards should be a little longer and extend higher than the outer boards so that the covering boards will lean outwards.

9. Cut and screw on covering boards E.

10. Now it's time to construct the door. Mount the horizontal braces F to the corner posts at the doorway with hinges on one end and temporarily with corner brackets on the other end.

Cut and mount the diagonals G.

Firmly screw in the boards on the inside and outside. These should reach down to the same level as the boards on the walls but not be quite the same height. Make sure that the boards for the door pass freely under the covering boards.

Remove the corner brackets and open the door.

*A fantastic feeling—
showering outside with
the sky as the ceiling!*

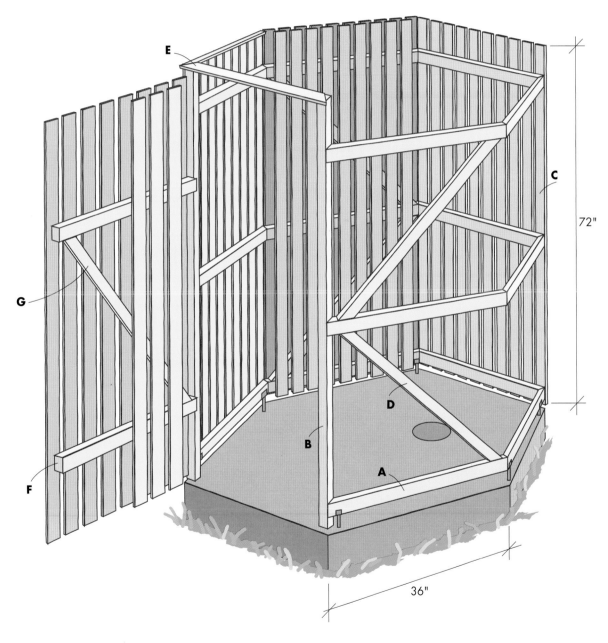

E

C

72"

G

D

B

F

A

36"

135

Fenced shed

The owner didn't leave anything to chance here. The shed is completely thought through, practical, and attractive. One section has a locking door and the rest just has a roof overhead. A privacy fence in the same style as the shed sturdily frames the lot. The fence line follows the slope of the ground and so, naturally, the fence height varies for a livelier design.

Materials for the shed

Pressure-treated cut wood, 4 x 4 (3½ x 3½")
    3 pieces each 94" (A1)
    3 pieces each 100" (A2)
    5 pieces each approx. 98" (A3)
    1 piece 82"(A4)

Pressure-treated wood, 2 x 4 (1½ x 3½")
    9 pieces each 92½" (B1)
    4 pieces each 168" (B2)
    3 pieces each 140½" (B3)
    1 piece 44½" (B4)
    1 piece 78" (B5)
    6 pieces each 14½"(B6)

2 x 8 (1½ x 7½"
    3 pieces each approx. 19'(C)

Unfinished tongue-and-groove, 1 x 4 (¾ x 3½")
    approx. 182 square feet (D)

Triangular edge molding, 5⅞ x 5⅞"
    2 pieces each approx. 19' (E)

Pressure-treated wood, 1 x 4 (¾ x 3½")
    2 pieces each approx. 9½' (F)

Pressure-treated wood, 1 x 6 (¾ x 5½")
    16 pieces each 76" (H1)
    63 pieces each 84" (H2)
    6 pieces each 94" (H3)
    approx. 125 running feet (H4 and H5)
    7 pieces each 72" (H6)

Pressure-treated cut wood, 1 x 2 (¾ x 1½")
    approx. 610 running feet (I1), (I2), (I3)

Plinths: 12
Hexagonal bolts, nuts, and washers for the plinths
Roofing felt and asphalt adhesive for
    approx. 17 square meters (G)
Roof foot plates: 2 pieces each 7'
Door
Nails
Roofing nails
Wood screws
Roofing Sheet Metal plates

Instructions for the shed

1. Set out the plinths (see "Foundations," page 105).

2. Cut the posts A1 (3 pieces), A2 (3 pieces) and A4 (1 piece) with all the joint notches and set them into place on the plinth post fasteners. (Set in one B to make it easier to get them all at the correct height.) Make sure that the posts are vertical.

3. Cut posts A3 (5 pieces) with the joint notches for B and set them in place temporarily. Mark their height with a stretched cord between A1 and A2. Take down, cut the tops, and set them in place again. Make sure that they are vertical. On the posts for the center roof beam C, the notch at the top should be made in the center, while the outer posts have joint notches for the roof beams C on the inside of the post.

4. Join all the B horizontal boards. Note that the top B on all the walls is obliquely cut on the top edge.

5. Cut the roof beams C, lay them into place, and screw them in securely.

6. Nail up the unfinished tongue-and-groove D. It should extend out the same amount on each end. Let the boards extend out a bit more than the finished measurements and then cut them cleanly afterwards.

7. Screw the triangular edge molding E securely to the underside of the unfinished tongue-and-groove boards D. Join the roof fascia boards F to the ends of C and E.

8. Nail on the roof foot plate securely and lay the roofing felt G on with roofing nails and asphalt glue (see instructions on the packaging).

9. Screw on panels H1, H2, H3, and H6 (H2, H3, and H6 are not included on the drawings), equally spaced in the partitions between posts A. The outermost boards should lie in towards the posts.

10. Screw on the boards H4 firmly up and down on all sides.

11. Securely screw the cover battens I1 between both H4 boards and over the grooves of panel H.

12. Firmly screw on the covering boards H5 above the top boards B.

13. Screw on rails I2 to support the panel rails I3 on the posts. Note that, on the long sides, I3 is partly screwed to roof beams C and partly into the short pieces of I2 that are connected to the posts A under the roof beam C.

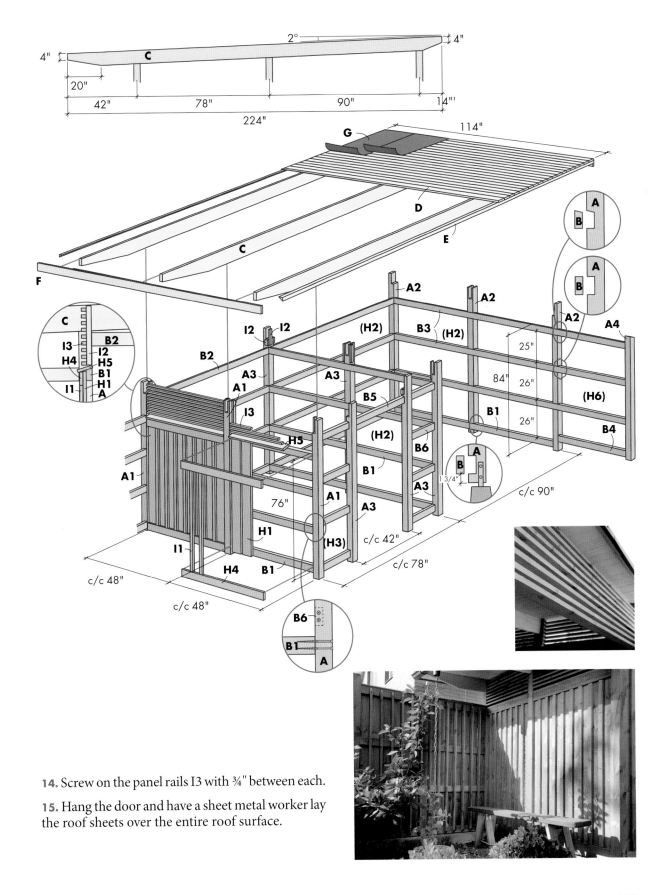

14. Screw on the panel rails I3 with ¾" between each.

15. Hang the door and have a sheet metal worker lay the roof sheets over the entire roof surface.

Materials for the privacy fence

The number of sections should be adjusted to the total length of the privacy fence. For this reason, the total amounts for materials have not been calculated below. If the ground slopes, construct the fence in steps that align with the slope of the ground.

Pressure-treated cut wood, 4 x 4 (3½ x 3½")
    82" (A). If the fence steps down, the posts will be higher at the transition between two different levels

Pressure-treated lumber 1 x 4 (¾ x 3½")
    lengths of 6' and 12' (B)

Pressure-treated wood, 1 x 5 (¾ x 4½")
    1 piece 68½" (C) per section
    15 pieces each 76" (D) per section
    2 pieces each 68½" (E) per section

Pressure-treated cut wood, 1 x 2 (¾ x 1½")
    15 pieces each 66½" (F) per section
    15 pieces each 76½" (G) per section

Plinths
Hexagonal bolts, washers, and nuts for the plinths
Wood screws

Instructions for the privacy fence

1. Set out the plinths (see "Foundations," page 105).

2. Cut posts A with the notches for the joints with horizontal boards B. The posts in the transition between two levels in the fence are made without notches for B. Note that the top board B is obliquely cut on the top side.

3. Mount posts A into the plinths together with the bottom boards B. Make sure that everything is squared.

4. Mount the remaining boards B. Use 6' and 12' lengths and make sure to join them alternately at A so that there are a maximum of two joins per post.

5. Screw the covering boards C firmly to the top boards B.

6. Screw on the panel boards D spaced equidistantly. The outermost ones should lie against posts A.

7. Mount boards E at the top and bottom of the panels.

8. Screw the cover rails F between the two E-boards and over the grooves of the panels.

9. Cut and screw on rails G into B, centered on the intermediate space between the panel boards D.

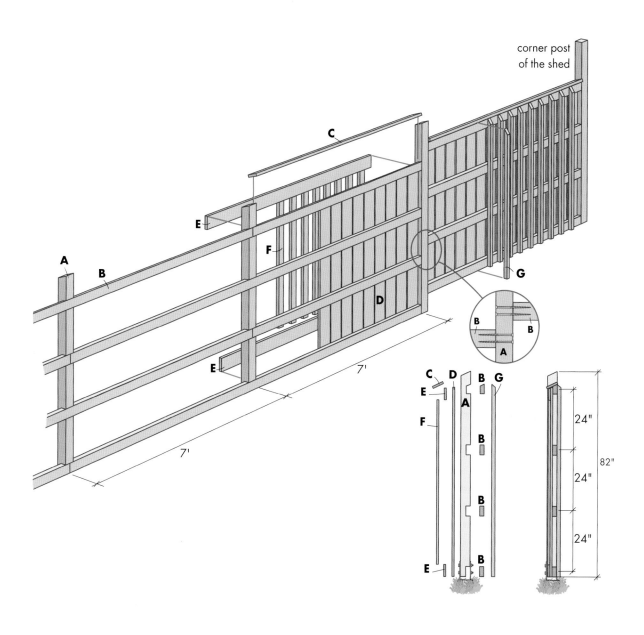

corner post
of the shed

C

E

A

B

F

D

E

G

B

B

A

7'

7'

C

D

B

G

E

A

F

B

B

B

E

B

24"

24"

24"

82"

*The rails are an attractive feature
that livens up the fence.*

Stairs & porches

Exterior wood steps must be usable in the summer as well as the winter. For that reason, it is important that they be constructed with the utmost care and the right materials. The principles are the same, whether it concerns stairs for an entryway, a terrace, or a freestanding staircase in the yard between varying ground levels.

A porch is a somewhat special construction that doesn't work on all houses. It is important to think about how the house will look with a porch, and in any case, how it should be shaped to blend in with the rest of the structure.

Planning

Begin by measuring the differences in level. Consider whether or not you will have a landing when coming up the stairs, or a "veranda" centered on the stairs if it is long. When it comes to an entryway, a larger landing might be preferable so that there is sufficient space for opening the door.

Think about the entirety of the house. A stairway is a part of the house or, if freestanding, a part of the yard.

Think about safety. Does it need a railing or handrail? Rough-sawn wood on flat stairs minimizes the risk of slipperiness.

To make things easier, you should first understand the general principles for building stairs. It is also good to know what the different parts are called (see figure below).

Additional considerations
• Choose high-quality pressure-treated wood for all the parts that come in contact with the ground, affect personal safety, and that are difficult to change out. For the other parts, choose a normal pressure-treated wood grade.
• All fittings, screws, bolts, and nails should, at the very least, be galvanized and completely rustproof.
• The stairs must be constructed so that water and moisture cannot pool on the steps but, instead, run off easily. Make sure that the riser leans slightly outwards so that water runs off the stairs.
• A staircase ought to have a slope angle of between 17° and 30°. Exterior stairs should have a smaller angle than an indoor staircase. The heights of the steps should be between 5½ and 7½". Walking up an exterior staircase usually seems more strenuous, so it is best that the step height not exceed 6". The depth of the steps should be at least 10", preferably 12".

The step height and step depth
are calculated following this formula:
2 × step height + step depth = 24".

Here's how you calculate the step height
For example:
The level of difference is 40"
Desired step height is max 6"

$40/6 = 6.67$ steps
Choose 7 steps for a step height of 5¾".

Here's how you calculate step depth
For example:
$2 × 5¾ + X = 24"$
$X = 12½"$ (step depth)

• The treads should use 2x stock (1½" thick) and the maximum span should be 16". For wider spans or thinner treads, add extra stringers.
• The handrail is set 36" above the step nose. A handrail should always be part of a steep staircase.
• For more information concerning stairs and porches, read the section, "Rules and Regulations" on page 104.

General Instructions
• For a staircase that will lie directly on the ground and follow the slope of the ground, lay the stringers on concrete tiles. In other situations, some form of plinth foundation must be used. Read more about "Foundations" on page 105.
• Even pressure-treated wood must be finished. Read more about "Finishing" on page 118.

Look at our examples and find inspiration.

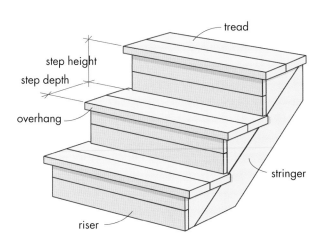

tread
step height
step depth
overhang
riser
stringer

Stairs

The family renovated the kitchen and used the opportunity to make a doorway out to the yard. A large and inviting stairway was constructed that very nicely connects the kitchen with the small yard. The stairs became a place to sit down with morning coffee in hand and eyes on the morning newspaper.

Materials

The entire structure is built on six stringers that were purchased ready-made at building suppliers.

Stringers (A): 6

2 x 6 (1½ x 5½")
    6 pieces legs (B) each approx. 24"
    1 support (C) 40"
    1 block (D) approx. 4"

Pressure-treated decking wood, 2 x 6 (1½ x 5½")", approx. 140':
    for the treads (E), the risers (F), and the cap (G)

2 x 2 (1½ x 1½")
    2 pieces each approx. 36" (H)

Nail plates: 6
Anchor screws
Wood screws
Roofing underlayment
Optional: garden paving stones, 7⅞ x 1¼', coarse gravel and setting sand

Instructions

Stairs should not be set directly on the ground or grass. The easiest solution is to place the stairway on a stone surface, so that all you need to do is start building. Otherwise, you'll need a foundation of concrete pavers, two pavers for every leg. Measure where the legs will be and then dig holes about 8" deep. Pour in 4" thick, coarse gravel, pack it down, and then pack sand down hard to make a 2" layer. Pour in setting sand and level it off. Set the pavers in place and use a level to make sure that all the stones are the same level. The pavers should lie at ground level.

1. With stringers A as the starting point, cut legs B to the correct angle and length. Join them with nail plates and anchor screws in each stringer.

2. Lay a strip of roofing underlayment under all the surfaces that come into contact with the ground.

3. Firmly screw on two of the leg fasteners in the support C, which will later rest against the house. There should be 24" between the legs. Set the support with the screwed-on fasteners in place against the wall.

4. Join a block D to the center of the support and hammer in a nail centered on the top side to mark the center of the step. The nail will be used when the remaining leg fasteners are set out.

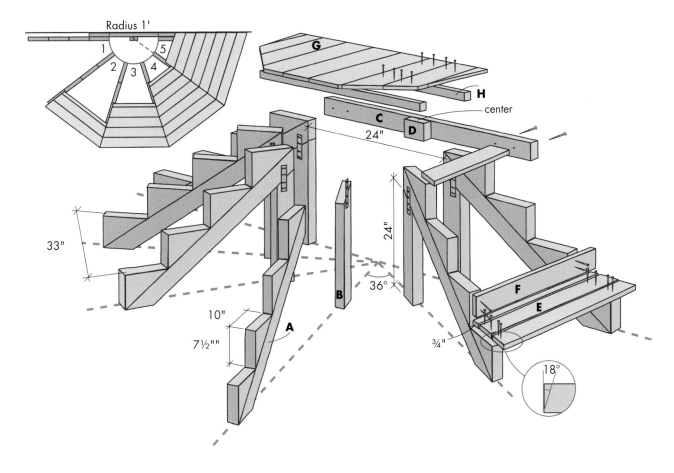

5. Measure and set all the angles; there should be 36° between the legs. The distance from each fastener to the center nail should be 12". Bore a hole in a piece of scrap lumber that the nail you put in D will go through, then cut off the board 12" from the hole and use this template when the legs are set out. Adjust the level of the leg fasteners with their respective steps. You might need to wedge under some spots to ensure that all the leg fasteners are level. Use the level and folding ruler and measure very carefully!

6. Cut and firmly screw on all the treads E. The angle on the ends should be 18°. Measure carefully! Measure each step—if the legs aren't in the precisely correct place, it won't matter too much. Just check and cut each step individually. The innermost board should be ripped to fit. Leave a gap of ⅛" between the boards. Note that the step nearest the house should go past the stringer by 1½" in order to reach into the wall.

Remove the rails that fixed the staircase afterwards, once the cladding is finished.

7. The staircase doesn't need to be connected to the wall. It will be stable enough, but it is also a good idea to attach it with screws through the supports and into the wall.

8. Cut the risers F (the angle at the ends should be 18°) and then screw them into place. Place them ⅜" above the tread.

9. Make a cap for the boards G and H and lay it into place. It doesn't need to be connected; it is a good idea to be able to lift it off if you lose something between the gaps.

Small entryway roof

The roof over the outer door doesn't need to be large in order for it to be functional. It makes the façade much nicer and you get protection from the rain while you unlock the door. The chain, which leads the water from the gutter down to the ground, feels totally right on this house.

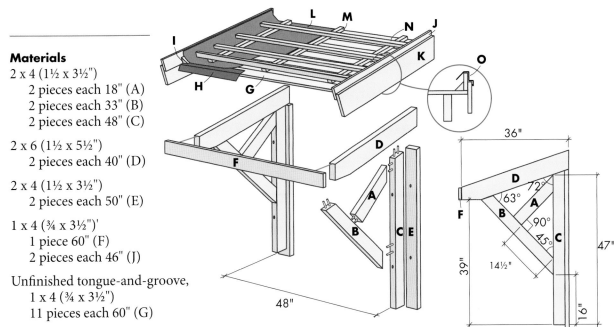

Materials

2 x 4 (1½ x 3½")
    2 pieces each 18" (A)
    2 pieces each 33" (B)
    2 pieces each 48" (C)

2 x 6 (1½ x 5½")
    2 pieces each 40" (D)

2 x 4 (1½ x 3½")
    2 pieces each 50" (E)

1 x 4 (¾ x 3½")'
    1 piece 60" (F)
    2 pieces each 46" (J)

Unfinished tongue-and-groove,
    1 x 4 (¾ x 3½")
    11 pieces each 60" (G)

Triangular rails, 2 x 2"
    2 pieces each 36"(I)

1 x 6 (¾ x 5½")
    2 pieces each 45" (K)

1 x 2, (¾ x 1½")
    3 pieces each 36" (M)
    4 pieces each 54" (N)

Roofing foot plate (H)
Roofing felt (L)
Wood pins for joining the brackets
Sheet metal (O)
Long French wood screws: 4
Wood screws
Roofing nails
Glue for exterior use
Gutter brackets
Rain gutter
Roofing underlay

Instructions

Finish all the parts before final assembly

1. Cut diagonal bars A on both ends and bar B on the lower end as shown in the drawing. Bore the holes for the pins, glue them together, place in a press, and let the glue dry.

2. Set A and B against C as in the drawing. Lay D on top. Mark for cutting on B, C, and D. Also mark on C where the hole for the installation should be bored. Cut parts B, C, and D. Hold C and E together, marking angle upwards on E, and cut. Place C and E together and bore the holes.

3. Glue together A/B with C and D. Glue and nail E to C.

4. Screw the complete brackets to the wall, using a level to make sure that it is precisely true.

5. Screw board F in securely and then the unfinished tongue-and-groove G to the boards D.

6. Countersink the gutter hooks in the tongue-in-groove; a circular saw will be useful here. Screw the gutter brackets into place and nail the roof foot plate H there.

7. Screw on the triangular rails I and fascia boards J and K in that order.

8. Lay on the roofing L and attach it with roofing nails.

9. Nail the counter laths M and then the support laths N. The distance between the N laths is determined by the roofing tiles.

10. Lay the roof tiles. Mount the gutter and sheet metal O. Finish with a drop edge of sheet metal against the house.

Small porch

This porch frames the door and makes the entry inviting and pleasant. It adds to the character of the house and, although the enclosed foundation only measures 18 square feet, it's large enough for a few potted plants. The porch keeps rain and snow well away from the hall and the recessed lighting in the ceiling provides a welcoming light when it is dark.

Materials

2 x 6 (1½ x 5½")
    1 piece 54½" (B)
    1 piece 54½" (C)
    1 piece 54½" (D)

2 x 5 (1½ x 4½")
    2 pieces each 88" (A)
    4 pieces each 40" (E)
    2 pieces each 69" (H)

2 x 2 (1½ x 1½")
    2 pieces each 12" (J)
    1 piece 45" (I)
    1 piece 29" (V)
    2 pieces each 54" (L)

2 x 3 (1½ x 3½")
    2 piece each 40" and
    2 pieces each 45½'" (X)

1 x 3 (¾ x 3½")
    25 pieces each 36" (Y)
    1 piece 40" and
    1 piece 45½" (Z)

1 x 8 (¾ x 7½")
    1 piece 71" (Q)
    2 pieces each 74" (P)

1 x 6 (¾ x 5½")
    2 pieces each 74" (O)

Unfinished tongue-and-groove, 1 x 4 (¾ x 3½")
    21 pieces each 71" (K)

2 x 5 (¾ x 4½")
    2 pieces each 88" (F)
    2 pieces each 93½" (G)

Triangular rails, 2 x 2"
    2 pieces each 69'" (N)

1 x 2 (¾ x 1½"), 44¼': (S and T)

Exterior paneling, approx. 125', but the amount
    will vary depending on the width of the panels.

Post fasteners
Corner brackets
Wood screws
Nails and roofing nails
Gutter brackets
Roof foot plate (M)

Roofing felt (R)
Roof tiles
Gutter
Sheet metal (U)

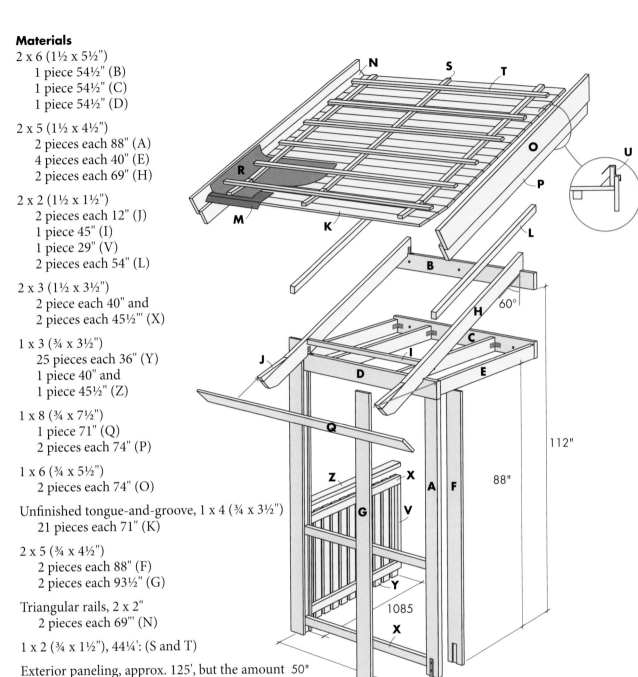

150

Instructions

Remember to finish all the pieces before final assembly.

1. Install the flat metal prongs as post fasteners in the ground or into the plinths. There should be 1½" between the fasteners in each corner.

2. Set up the posts A and screw them firmly into the post fasteners with through hexagonal bolts, washers, and nuts. Trim the screws even with the nuts.

3. Screw boards B to the wall, using an expanding bolt or the type of bolt suitable for the wall.

4. Screw the frame of the lower roof together with corner brackets and pieces C, D, and 4 pieces of E.

5. Set the frame on the posts A, use a level to make sure all the parts are true, and screw it securely to the wall.

6. Chisel the recesses for the fasteners in the covering boards F and G and screw them in. G holds D together and posts A. Note that G should extend 3¾" above the top edge of D.

7. Cut the roof boards H and attach them with corner brackets to B and D. H is then attached to G. Firmly screw rail I between the roof boards H directly above D.

8. Cut the wedges J so that they are 1½" high at the front edge and then screw them firmly into the top side of the roof boards H.

9. Nail up the tongue-and-groove K. Screw rails L under K. The paneling will be screwed into rails L so that they are placed at the center above the outer boards E in the frame.

10. Countersink the holes for the gutter brackets in the tongue-and-groove, preferably using a circular saw. Screw the gutter brackets into place and nail the roof foot plate there.

11. Screw on the triangular rails N and the wind boards O and P in that order.

12. Screw the covering board Q in firmly.

13. Lay the roofing felt R and secure it with roofing nails.

14. Nail on the counter laths S and the support laths T. The distance between the support laths is determined by the roof tiles.

15. Lay the roof tiles. Mount the gutters and the sheet metal U. Finish with a drop edge of sheet metal against the house.

16. Screw on board V to the house wall.

17. Join boards X to V and F on one gable and, respectively, in the two covering boards F on the front. Use small corner brackets or screw in diagonally.

18. Arrange the rails Y and screw them in securely to horizontal boards X. They should be spaced approx. ¾" apart.

19. Screw on the covering boards Z.

20. Screw on the lower roof and then the panels on the gables and front. The panels should extend down approx. ¾".

151

Inviting entryway

The built-in bench, the steps going in two directions, and the pretty roof make this entryway one of the most inviting you can imagine. Of course, the large, green, wooden house with its red trim helps to make the picture perfectly complete; however, the idea of an entry itself is perfectly applicable to other houses.

Stairs with a bench

Materials

All the wood is pressure-treated except for the painted banister (F, J, K, L).

4 x 4 (3½ x 3½")
  3 pieces each 18" (A)
  2 pieces each 67" (F)

2 x 4 (1½ x 3½")
  2 pieces each 163" (B1)
  2 pieces each 64" (B2)
  2 pieces each 61" (B3)
  2 pieces each 9½" (B4)

2 x 7 (1½ x 6½")
  4 pieces each 15" (C1)
  2 pieces each 64" (C2)
  2 pieces each 61" (C3)
  1 piece 119" (C4)
  4 pieces each 9½" (C5)
  2 pieces each 108" (E1)
  2 pieces each 49" (E2)
  2 pieces each 46" (E3)
  4 pieces each 9½" (E4)
  2 pieces each 47½" (G1)
  3 pieces each 86" (G2)

2 x 3 (1½ x 2½")
  14 pieces each 9½" (D1)
  2 pieces each 10½" (D2)
  2 pieces, each 101" (J)

2 x 6 (1½ x 5½")
  2 pieces each 101" (H)

Decking wood, 5/4 x 4 (1" x 3½"), approx. 330' (I)

2 x 2 (1½ x 1½")
  21 pieces each 27" (K)

2 x 4 (1½ x 3½")
  2 pieces each 101" (L)

2 x 4 (1½ x 3½")
  2 pieces each 22" (N1)
  2 pieces each 14" (N2)
  2 pieces each 6" (N3)
  2 pieces each 16¼" (M)

Plinths: 3
Hexagonal bolts, washers, and nuts for the plinths
French wood screws, nail plugs or fasteners appropriate for the façade: 8
Carriage bolts: 8
Corner brackets
Nail plates
Anchor screws
Wood screws
Glue for exterior use

Instructions

1. Set out the three plinths with the center 60" from the house (see "Foundations" on page 105).

Mount the posts A in the plinths with screws, washers, and nuts. The outside edge is 60¾" from the house.

2. Screw boards B1 firmly to the posts and then to the house. Use a board and level to make sure that everything is at the same height and is true.

3. Screw on boards B2 firmly. Attach B3 with corner brackets. Screw on B4 securely.

4. Screw C1 firmly to the posts at the front and attach with nail plates to B1 at the house. Screw C4 firmly to the posts and then to the house. Screw C2 (4 pieces) on firmly. Attach C3 (6 pieces) with corner brackets and then screw on C5 (4 pieces) firmly.

5. Attach E1 to the house with nail plates in C4 and then screw E2 securely to it. Screw the outer board E1 firmly between E2.

6. Profile cut a 4¾" high point at the top of the posts F and cut the notches for E1. Attach the posts to E1 and C3 with carriage bolts. Use a level to make sure that they are vertical.

7. Join G2 with nail plates to E1 at the house, screw G1 firmly to G2. Next, attach the 2 pieces of G2 between the two G1 boards, at the outside and then the middle. Mount a board I with the notch for F above the outer board E1 and then screw H firmly to the outer horizontal G2.

8. Screw rails D1 firmly in the ends of the steps and then mount boards D2 at a 45° angle at posts A.

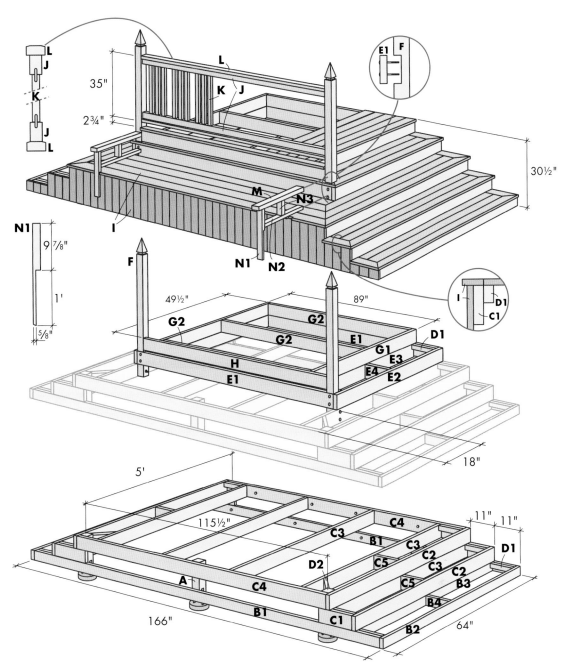

9. Clad the surfaces with decking I. Begin at the front because the steps and seat will go over these.

10. Join the fence rails K to horizontals J with wood plugs and glue. Set in a press and let glue dry. In this case, the rails are mounted in groups of three.

11. Plane down the edges of covering boards L and then screw them firmly into J. Set the finished fence in place and screw it in firmly with long screws through F.

12. Cut the uprights N1. Make a notch in the front edge on the outer seat board I just where N1 will be joined. Screw N1 firmly to the upright panel I.

13. Screw M, N2, and N3 together and set them into place. Screw M and N2 firmly into N1. Diagonally screw M and N2 into F and E1.

Entry roof

Materials

2 x 4 (1½ x 3½")
    1 piece 69" (A1)
    2 pieces each 22" (A2)
    2 pieces each 30" (A3)
    1 piece 28" (A4)
    4 pieces each 18" (A5)
    2 pieces each 41" (A6)
    2 pieces each 24" (B1)
    2 pieces each 33½" (B2)
    1 piece 31½" (B3)
    2 pieces each 45" (C)
    2 pieces each 39" (D)
    4 pieces each 53" (E)
    1 piece 13¾" (F)

½" Plywood, approx. 1½ sheets, each 4 x 8' (G)

Double tongue-and-groove, 1 x 5 (¾ x 5½"),
    approx. 66" (H)

Decorative molding 2", approx. 12' (I)

Roofing felt and asphalt adhesive
    for approx. 43 square feet
Roofing nails
French wood screws or screws appropriate
    for the façade
Corner brackets
Wood screws

Instructions

1. The lower frame (A1-A6) can be built on the ground. Cut all the pieces. Boards A2, A3, and A4 are cut at a 22.5° angle on the angled corners. The stiffeners A5 are cut at a 22.5° angle (see drawing).

2. Join A1 and A2 with screws and corner brackets. Continue, screwing the parts together using A5. Finish by screwing A6 in firmly, which must be notched on the front edge for A5.

3. Cut pieces B1, B2, and B3, also cutting at a 22.5° angle. Screw them securely, from the inside, to the outer part of frame A.

4. Screw the frame into place. Wedge under the frame until it is in at a 90° angle. Cut parts C and join them to the façade. You can most easily determine the angles by measuring while holding up the boards in the right place and marking them.

5. Join the diagonals D to boards A6 using screws and corner brackets on both sides of C.

6. Join the roof boards E. In this case, it is also easiest to get the angles correct by measuring in place or holding the work piece up and marking. The support board F is screwed in to support boards E.

7. Measure in place and cut sheets G and screw them on.

8. Screw panels H to the underside of the roof. Cut the decorative rails with a 22.5° angle for the corners and screw them into place.

9. Attach the roofing felt with roofing nails and asphalt glue. Leave the sheet metal work to a specialist.

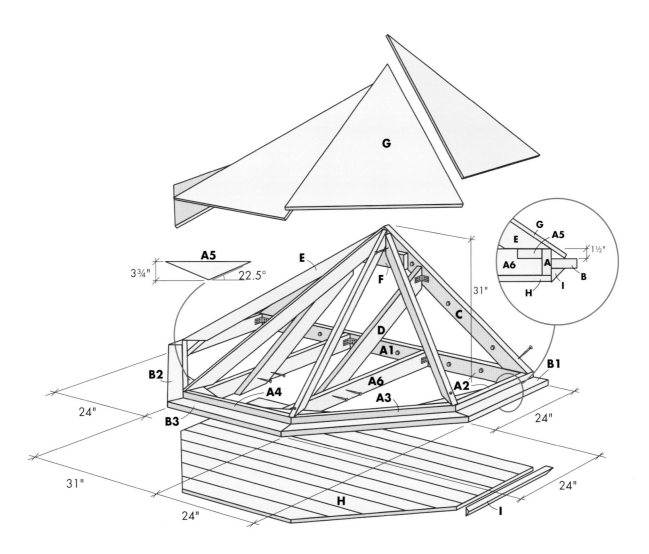

G

A5
3¾"   22.5°

E

F

C

31"

D

A1

B2

A6   A2

A4

B3   A3   B1

24"

24"

31"

24"   H   24"

I

G   A5
E
A6   A   1½"
H   I   B

A solid roof was needed to complete the picture for this magnificent entryway.

157

Garden furniture

Garden furniture is very appealing. Besides all the traditional retail stores, there are many specialty shops that have begun catering to our increased interest in the yard in the past few years. Despite that, you might still have difficulty finding the furniture that is just right for you, your budget, or your yard. If you can do the carpentry work yourself, you can make furniture that suits your situation. You can also make pieces that fold down easily for winter storage.

Many people think cooking outdoors is wonderful on a warm summer evening. The outdoor kitchens sold in stores most often include a large grill fired by propane in addition to built-in stove tops and work surfaces—everything for a prodigious amount of money. Why not construct the outdoor kitchen yourself? You can build it according to your needs and pocketbook.

Leaf through the following pages for inspiration.

Garden table

Southern Europe, sun, vacation, good food and drink with the best of friends! This is the essence that we wanted to embrace with this rustic garden table. The table is constructed with pine lumber and painted burnt umber with oil paint from a tube. It is a table with a pleasing weight that also folds down and can be put away when winter comes.

Materials

2 x 6 (1½ x 6½")
    5 pieces each 84" (A)
    1 piece 84" (D)
    4 pieces each 43½" (C)

2 x 2 (1½ x 1½")
    2 pieces each 27½" (B)

1 x 5 for the wedges, a harder
    wood recommended (preferably oak)
    2 pieces each 10" (E)

Wood screws: 20
Wood glue for exterior use
Paint suitable for exterior use

Instructions

1. Cut pieces A and B for the table top. Glue and screw them together. The supports B should be placed 6" from the ends of A.

2. Rough-cut legs C. Draw rectangles based on the cross measurements (see blue dash lines). Set the pieces for the legs in a rectangle and mark the placement of the recesses for the lap joints.

3. Using a circular saw, cut the halving joints half the depth of the wood for the legs. Make multiple cuts and then chisel the rest away.

4. Set the pieces together; they should fit rather tightly. Glue, clamp, and let dry.

5. Arrange the finished cross in a rectangle again (blue dash lines) and mark the leg lengths and angles. Cut.

6. Draw the holes, 1½ x 2½", at the center of the leg crosses. Bore several holes and then chisel out each hole.

7. Cut horizontal D that connects the leg crosses, with a 6" long x 2½ wide tenon at each end.

8. Bore and chisel out the holes for the wedges E.

9. Cut the wedges and assemble the table.

Because of the weight of the table top and the stability of the supports, they don't have to be attached to each other. This makes the table easy to take down and store away during the winter. If you want, though, you can screw a couple of screws into the table top boards B and into the legs, or make a couple of round wood tenons that can easily be removed.

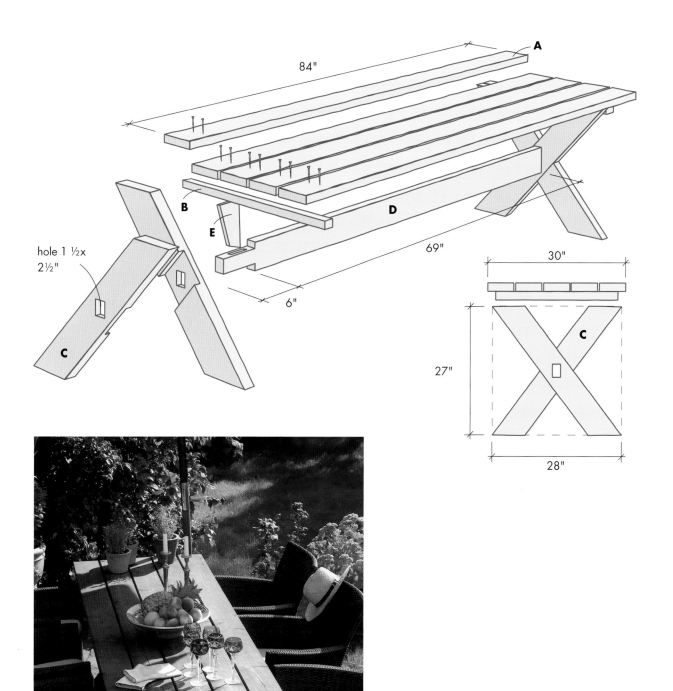

84"

A

hole 1 ½x
2½"

B

C

E

D

69"

6"

30"

27"

C

28"

By blending burnt umber oil paint from a tube, boiled linseed oil, and a few drops of siccative, we made the table a pleasing shade of brown. Blend the paint to the consistency of buttermilk in a glass jar, drop on a few daubs with a brush and then take a rag and rub the paint in evenly. Done! A simple and flexible way to paint the table so it will stay fresh for a long time.

163

Small bench

You can't have too many benches in the yard. You can set them in various spots, so you can stand up, sit down, and take a break almost anywhere. This photo shows a small, pretty bench that is slightly curved for increased seat comfort, and has good-sized feet for stability. The feet also contribute to the bench's very fine proportions.

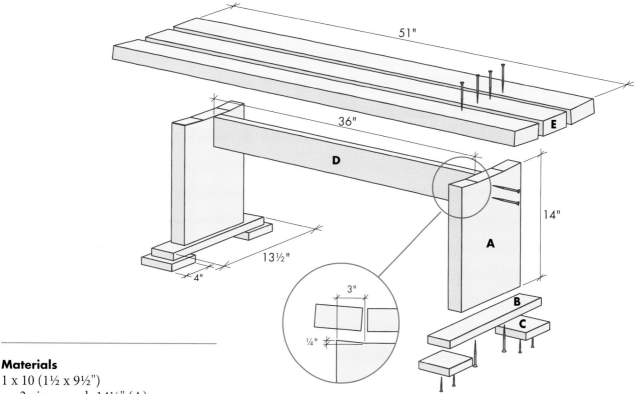

Materials

1 x 10 (1½ x 9½")
    2 pieces each 14½" (A)

1 x 3 (¾ x 2½") pressure treated
    2 pieces each 13½"(B)

1 x 4 (¾ x 3½") pressure treated
    4 pieces each 4" (C)
    1 piece 36" (D)

2 x 4 (1½ x 3½")
    3 pieces each 51" (E)

Wood screws
Glue for exterior use
Exterior paint

Instructions

1. Cut legs A. Cut a profile along the top edge with a jigsaw (see drawing).

2. Cut the base of the legs B and feet C. Glue and screw them together and then glue and screw B to legs A.

3. Cut the support rail D that sits between the legs. Glue and screw it in firmly.

4. Cut the seat boards E. Sand the ends of the wood and round the edges. Also round the long sides for better seating comfort. Glue and screw them into place, leaving room between the slats, and overhanging the legs.

Finishing
Oil all the parts, coating particularly well on the ends of the wood. Let the oil dry. Apply two coats of primer, sand lightly, and finish with a coat of exterior enamel.

165

Outdoor kitchen

It's so nice to visit with your family and friends while cooking. With an outdoor kitchen you avoid being left alone in the kitchen while the guests socialize outside in the beautiful weather. This brown-stained outdoor kitchen has a divided bench shelf made partly from plywood, partly with tiles. The round, stainless steel wash pan is set into the shelf and the drainage problem is easily solved with a bucket. The shelf at the top serves double duty as a bar where your friends can stand and hang out with aperitifs.

Materials

2 x 3 (1½ x 2½")
>   2 pieces each 36"(A)
>   2 pieces each 52" (B)
>   5 pieces each 21" (C)
>   2 pieces each 23¾" (D)
>   3 pieces each 65" (F)
>   1 piece 44" (G)

2 x 2 (1½ x 1½")
>   2 pieces each 19" (E)
>   1 piece 18½" (H)
>   4 pieces each 21" (I)
>   2 pieces each 9" (J)

1 x 5 (¾ x 4½")
>   4 pieces each 72"(K)
>   2 pieces each 72" (L)
>   5 pieces each 47½" (N)

1 x 2 (¾ x 1½")
>   3 pieces each 8" (M)
>   1 piece 72" (Q)
>   approx. 16" (R)

1 x 3 (¾ x 2½") for the tray S,
>   approx. 13'

$^{11}/_{32}$" exterior plywood
>   24 x 41" (P)

Ceramic tiles, 12 x 12" (O): 4
Corner brackets: 9
Nail plates: 1
Wood screws
Glue for exterior use
Set-in wash pan

Instructions

1. Cut parts A, B, C, and D for both ends. Glue and screw them together. Also attach rail E that the table top will rest on. It should be approx. 19" long, but the length depends on the size of the corner brackets which are fastened at the corner.

2. Cut horizontal boards F and screw to the ends using corner brackets.

3. Cut pieces G, C, and H for the bottom shelf. Join G and C with corner brackets and mount the frame at F and A with corner brackets. The corner upright H, which holds the shelf up, is screwed in from underneath to G and then attached upwards with nail plates to F.

4. Cut, glue and screw the crosspieces I, which hold the shelf P, tiles O and, boards N to the lower shelf. Make sure that the two left boards for the work space are placed correctly. Press the tiles against board D and mark two tile widths on F. Place the crossbars in the middle, centered on the markings.

5. Cut the brackets J for the upper shelf. Glue and screw them into place.

6. Cut boards K for the back and screw them firmly into B from the back.

7. Construct the upper shelf with the two boards L and the three rails M. Glue and screw the parts together, lay the shelf in place, and screw it down well.

8. Cut boards N for the lower shelf and screw them securely to the frame.

9. Lay the tiles O loosely on the boards.

10. Cut the form plywood sheets P, making sure that they fit. Cut the hole for the wash pan and set the plywood sheet loosely in place.

11. Cut rails Q and glue and firmly screw on the one that edges the front on front board F.

12. Make the brackets R for the tray/side shelf. The height should be ⅜" less than the distance between boards C in the gables. Screw a strong screw in each end of the uprights on the brackets. Trim the screws with an angle grinder or hacksaw so that the lower screw has about should extend out ¼" showing and the top one approx. 1". Bore two holes on the underside of the top board C and the top side of the lower board. Set the brackets into place; they now pivot.

13. Cut the parts for the tray S. The two rails on the sides should be ripped so that they are 2" high. Cut a notch in the end rails so these are also 2" high at the center. Glue and screw the frame together. Glue and nail the bottom rails on securely.

14. Remove the tiles O and the plywood sheet P and finish the entire construction. We have coated it with exterior stain. Stain all the wood ends on the plywood sheet P.

15. Place the wash pan in the hole and then put the plywood sheet and the tiles back on.

16. Screw on the hooks wherever you think they are needed.

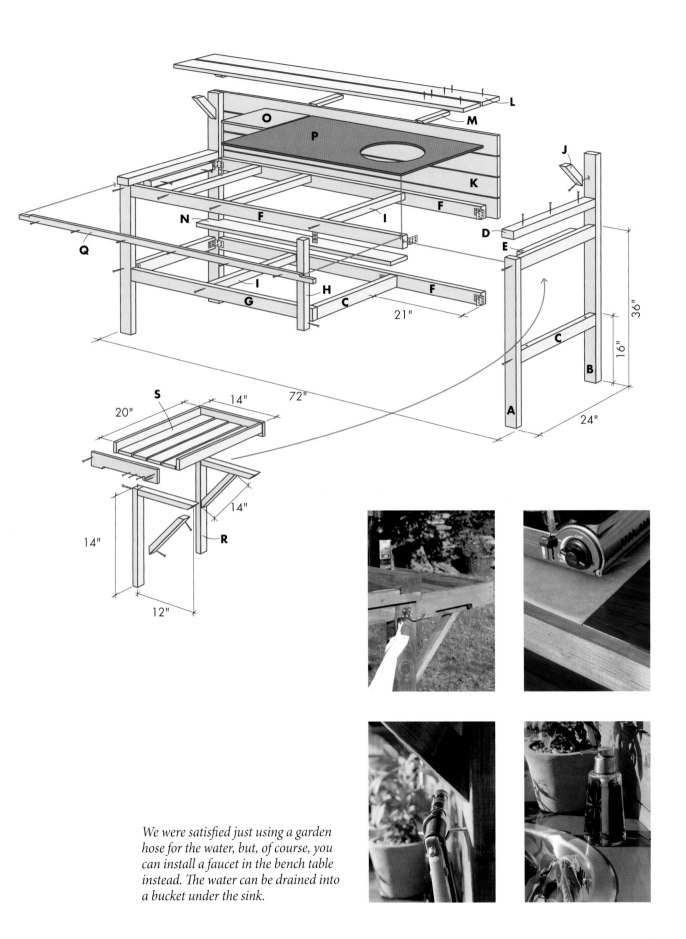

L

M

O

P

J

K

F

N

F

I

D

E

Q

I

H

F

G

C

C

21"

72"

36"

16"

B

A

24"

S

14"

20"

14"

R

14"

12"

We were satisfied just using a garden hose for the water, but, of course, you can install a faucet in the bench table instead. The water can be drained into a bucket under the sink.

Bench attached to wall

You can take a well-deserved break from yard work on this bench. The red paint gives the bench a nice color spark that contrasts well with the dark wall.

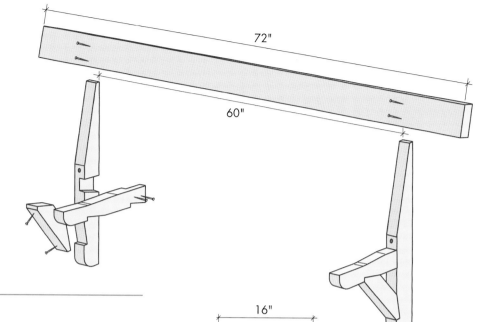

Materials

2 x 3 (1½ x 3½")
    2 pieces each 30" (A)
    2 pieces each 16" (B)
    2 pieces each 12" (C)

2 x 6 (1½ x 5½")
    3 pieces each 18" (D and E)

Wood screws
Glue for exterior use
Screws for hanging: 2 (In this case, the bench is mounted to the side of a shed and is hung with through carriage bolts. Use bolts/screws that are suitable for the wall.)

Instructions

1. Cut the two back uprights A. The top of the brackets should be ½" thick.

2. Cut the wedge shapes on one end of the support B, the cut edge to half thickness on the outside edge.

3. Round B on the front end and curve the top surface for the seat boards. It is ⅜" lower at the center of the two seat boards.

4. Lay the supports B over the back uprights A and mark where these should be cut. Cut A and chisel to half thickness.

5. Bore holes for the hangers in back uprights A.

6. Round off the uprights A at the bottoms and the supports B on the outer edges. The radius is 2".

7. Set A and B together, making sure the corners are squared. Lay the diagonal C over them at a 45° angle and mark the cutting lines.

8. Cut the recesses for C in both A and B. Lay A and B together again, at a right angle, now with C underneath. Mark how C should be cut on the ends. Cut C and put the pieces together; you might need to adjust a little with a file before the final assembly.

9. Glue and join parts A, B, and C into two brackets. (The construction is very stable, and can actually hold together without glue or screws.)

10. Mount the brackets on the wall.

11. Screw the seat boards D and the back boards E on securely.

12. We recommend that you finish the brackets and seat and back boards before the final assembly.

171

Tree bench

A classic—a bench around a large tree! What a lovely feeling, to find yourself in the shade of a big leafy tree on a warm summer day. When it's raining, why not sit huddled up facing the trunk? There is something cozy and secure in wooden benches—a little like building a cabin.

Materials

The bench fits around a tree up to approx. 6' in circumference or approx. 2' in diameter. All the wood is pressure treated.

2 x 3 (1½ x 2½")

4 x 4 (3½ x 3½")
    4 pieces each 19" (B)

1 x 4 (¾ x 3½") decking wood
    8 pieces each 20" (C)
    8 pieces each approx. 26" (D)
    40 pieces in varying lengths (E)

Wood screws
Corner brackets: 8

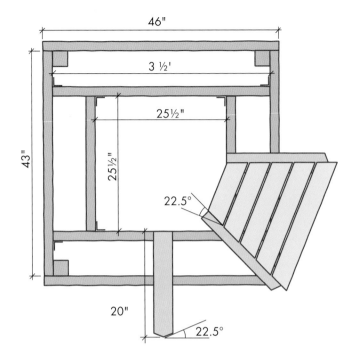

Instructions

The bench is easier to construct than you might believe when you see it finished. However, it is almost a necessity to have a crosscut and miter saw because there are so many 22.5° angles to cut.

1. Cut the pieces for frame A and join them with screws and corner brackets, using long (at least 3") screws in the corners. Measure carefully, because everything else depends on these sections being absolutely true and square.

2. Cut the legs B and attach them to the frame with long screws.

3. Cut and firmly screw on the seat board supports C; counterbore and use long screws (3"). Measure so that the distance between the boards directly opposite each other is 25½".

4. Measure the space between the points of the supports C. If everything is totally square, the pieces should be spaced equally apart, but presumably there could be small differences that won't matter. Measure, cut, and assemble the frame parts D one by one. The ends you cut first should have a 22.5° angle. Counterbore and attach the frame to the ends of the supports C with screws. To make the structure even stronger, you can tighten the screws in the corner on frame A.

5. Cut one end at a 22.5° angle on 5 pieces of the seat boards D. Set them into place, so that the outer ones extend out about ⅜". Use a ruler or straight board to mark where you should cut on the other end. Counterbore and attach the seat boards to the supports C. Use short screws that won't go through both boards. Continue the same way all around. Finally, you can tighten some screws by the outer seat boards and in the frame.

When I constructed the tree bench, I made it completely in the garage. Then I numbered the parts on the underside, took the bench apart, put the pieces around the tree, and assembled them *in situ*. That way, it was easier to measure and ensure that all the parts were true and straight.

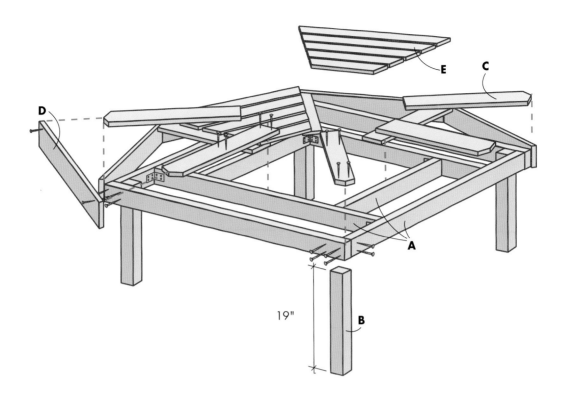

E

C

D

A

19"

B

Classic garden furniture

It has become quite popular to buy and renovate old garden furniture. However, the prices on the resale market have risen in step with the demand, and sometimes the furniture is in really bad shape. In that case, it is worth making the pieces yourself. You only need a little carpentry experience to construct this garden furniture and, while it is not a job done in record time, the knowledge that "I made it myself" makes it well worthwhile.

Materials for a chair

The dimensions given for A and B are slightly larger than the finished measurements to allow for adjustments.

1 x 4 (¾ x 3½")
    2 pieces each 42" (A)

1 x 3 (¾ x 2½")
    2 pieces each 26''' (B)
    2 pieces ach 18" (C)

1 x 2 (¾ x 1½")
    4 pieces each 16" (D, E and G)

1 x 3 (¾ x 2½")
    1 piece 17½" (F)

1 x 2 (¾ x 1½")
    10 pieces, the shortest 13½"
    and the longest 17" (H)

Carriage bolts with washers and self-locking nuts: 4
Wood screws
Glue for exterior use
Exterior paint

Instructions for the chair

Before assembling all the parts, sand them and bevel all the edges and corners. Counterbore and join the pieces with glue and screws. Throughout, work carefully and check to make sure everything is squared and level with a square rule.

1. Cut pieces A, B, and C.

2. Bore thin holes for the placement of the carriage bolts (B toward C and B towards A), and mount the parts temporarily with thin nails instead of bolts. Lay out one side of the chair in a row for a model and to make adjustments. Mark exactly where the braces D (1 piece) and E (2 pieces) will be placed.

3. Cut and chisel out the recesses for the back boards F and G in the back uprights A.

4. Cut the back boards F, G and 2 supports E and glue and screw them firmly to A.

5. Cut brace D; glue and screw it securely to B.

6. Join the two assembled parts together temporarily using nails and check everything before you bore and assemble the chair with screws. Note that there should be a washer between C and A as well as between C and B.

7. Cut the seat slats H a little larger than the final dimensions. Attach them temporarily, spacing them equidistantly and partially inserting the screws. Mark where they should be cut; the six back ones align with the side on C and the four front ones widen in a soft curve. Cut and join them with glue and screws.

8. Unscrew the carriage bolts and finish the three parts separately.

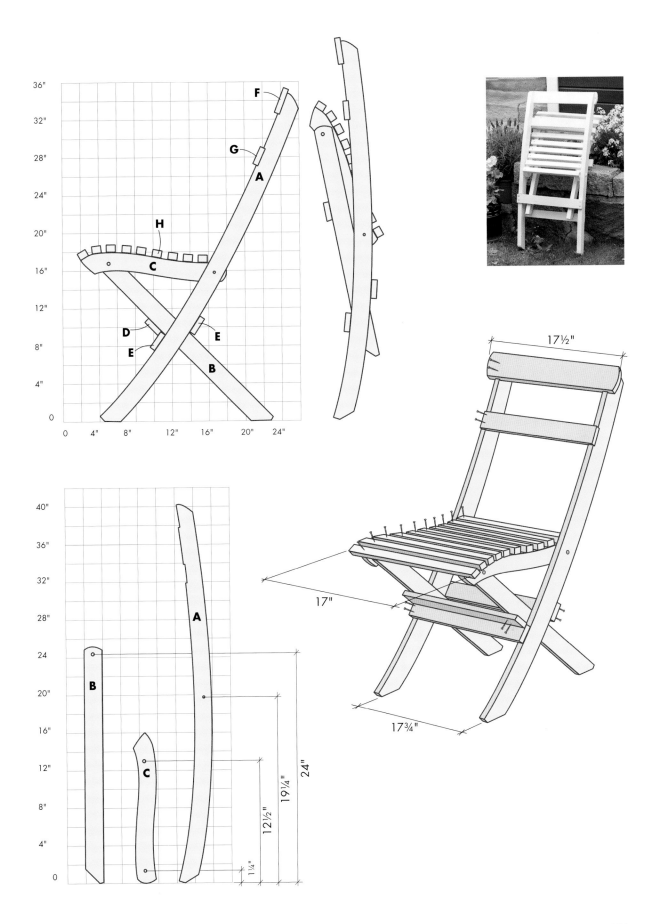

36"
32"
28"
24"
20"
16"
12"
8"
4"
0

F
G
A
H
C
D
E
E
B

0   4"   8"   12"   16"   20"   24"

40"
36"
32"
28"
24"
20"
16"
12"
8"
4"
0

A
B
C

24"
19¼"
12½"
1¼"

17½"
17"
17¾"

179

Materials for the table

The dimensions given for A and B are slightly larger than the finished measurements to allow for adjustments.

1 x 2 (¾ x 1½")
    2 pieces each 39½" (A)
    2 pieces each 39½" (B)

1 x 4 (¾ x 3½")
    2 pieces each 27" (C)

1 x 2 (¾ x 1½")
    1 piece 31½" (D)

1 x 3 (¾ x 2½")
    2 pieces each 4½" (E)
    2 pieces each 31½" (F)
    1 piece 30" (G)

1 x 2 (¾ x 1½")
    1 piece 33½" (H)

1 x 3 (¾ x 2½")
    9 pieces each 45" (J)

Carriage bolts with washers and self-locking nuts: 4
Wood screws
Glue for exterior use
Exterior paint

Instructions for the table

Before assembling all the parts, sand them and bevel all the edges and corners. Counterbore and join the pieces with glue and screws. Throughout, work carefully and check to make sure everything is squared and level with a square rule.

1. Cut pieces A, B, and C, leaving A and B extra long at the lower end.

2. Cut blocks E, but wait to cut the notches.

3. Lay out a pair of legs, A and B, as well as boards C and the blocks E, and adjust the measurements. The holes connecting B and C should be ¾" from the lower edge and approx. 4¾" from the end at C. On leg B, a second hole is centered about 1" from the end.

4. Bore thin holes for the placement of the carriage bolts (B towards C and B towards A), and mount the parts temporarily with thin nails instead of the bolts so that you can adjust the placement of the holes. Mark exactly where the rails G (1 piece) and F (2 pieces) will sit. Also mark precisely where blocks E will be placed and draw the notch, keeping in mind that rail D will sit in the notch.

5. Measure and draw the ends of the legs that will be on the ground. Cut them.

6. Make the notches in blocks E and mount them on board C.

7. Bore holes for the carriage bolts.

8. Glue and firmly screw support G to both legs A and then supports F (2 pieces) to both legs B. (The leg pair A will be placed inside of legs B.)

9. Glue and screw rail D firmly to both legs A. D should extend out ¾" on each side.

10. Connect the leg pairs A and B and boards C with the carriage bolts. Note that there should be a washer between A and B as well as between C and F.

11. Cut and join the diagonal H. First fold the table down and mark the placement for the top of the brace in the notch on block E when the table is folded together.

12. Glue and screw the table top slats J on firmly, spacing them equidistantly. Begin with the two outermost slats and then the one in the center, and then space the others.

13. Round the corners.

14. Disassemble and finish each of the three parts separately.

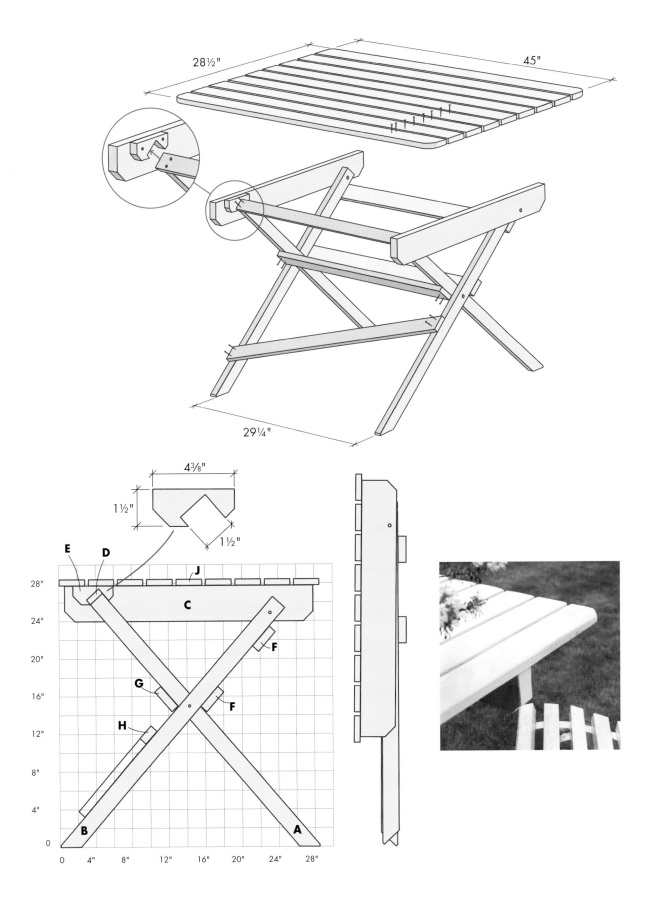

28½"

45"

29¼"

4⅜"

1½"

1½"

E

D

J

28"

C

24"

F

20"

G

16"

F

12"

H

8"

4"

B

A

0

0   4"   8"   12"   16"   20"   24"   28"

Liar's bench

In the little harbor, among the fishing sheds and piers, we found the model for this liar's bench. It was easy to imagine all the fishermen who, over the years, sat there and bragged about one "biggest" fish after another. The bench fits just as well in a yard—and you can even "tell a whopper" there.

Materials

1 x 8 (¾ x 7½")
   1 piece 72" (A)
   2 pieces each 16" (B)

2 x 2 (1½ x 1½")
   2 pieces each 7½"(C)

1 x 4 (¾ x 3½")
   2 pieces each 72" (D)

2 x 3 (1½ x 2½")
   2 pieces each 9½" (E)

Wood screws
Glue for exterior use
Exterior paint

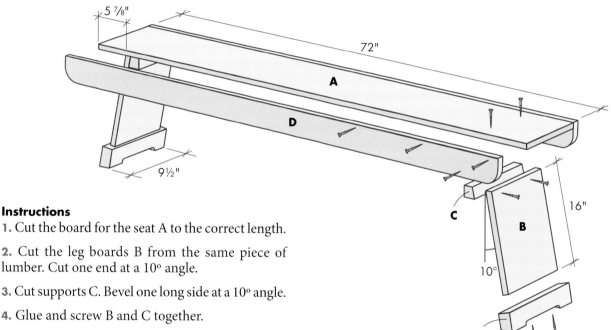

Instructions

1. Cut the board for the seat A to the correct length.

2. Cut the leg boards B from the same piece of lumber. Cut one end at a 10° angle.

3. Cut supports C. Bevel one long side at a 10° angle.

4. Glue and screw B and C together.

5. Glue and screw these firmly to the seat A, 6" from the ends.

6. Cut sides D, rounding off the ends as shown in the drawing.

7. Glue and screw the sides firmly to the bench. It is important that they are also attached to the legs.

8. Cut the feet E. Bevel one long side of the narrow edge at a 10° angle. Cut a recess about 1" deep in the angled, lower edge.

9. Turn the bench upside down and glue and screw the feet securely to the legs B.

10. Sand the seat surface and sides (it is easiest to do this with a belt sander).

11. Finish the bench appropriately.

Acknowledgments

When we started work on the book, we made lists of the desired projects that we wanted to have in it to try to cover as much as possible under the title *Outdoor Carpentry*. We made many of the projects in the book ourselves but, to attain our goal of making the book as wide-reaching as possible, we spent some time seeking out additional projects.

We want to thank all the wonderful and positive people that we met while working on the book and who contributed their own fine projects.

Here are some of the projects we found:
Björn and Lotta Andersson's skateboard ramp on page 94.
Peter Bengmark built his terrace around a large oak on the lot, see page 42.
Peter Johansson sketched the bicycle shed on page 122 and the large terrace on page 34.
Bo Lindkvist's inviting pier can be seen on page 96.
Börje Olofsson constructed the playhouse shown on page 126 many years ago and now it is the third generation's turn to take over the sweet cottage.
Gun and Claes-Olaf Olsson built the wind break on page 70.
André Waldhör designed and crafted the "Outdoor Room Divider" on page 74 as well as the firewood rack on page 130.

And to everyone else—thanks once more!

Anna and Anders Jeppsson
Hans-Ove Ohlsson

Translation by Omicron Language Solutions, LLC
Photography: Anna Jeppsson and Han-Ove Ohlsson
Drawings: Anders Jeppsson
Graphic design: Anna and Anders Jeppsson
Previously published in Swedish under the title *Snickra Ute* by Ica Book Publishers, Forma Books AB
©2009 Anna and Anders Jeppsson, Hans-Ove Ohlsson

Other Schiffer Books by the Author:
Basic Carpentry and Interior Design Projects for the Home and Garden: Make It Yourself.
Anna and Anders Jeppsson
978-0-7643-4363-6. $29.99

Other Schiffer Books on Related Subjects:
Espalier Fruit Trees For Wall, Hedge, and Pergola: Installation, Shaping, & Care.
Karl Pieber
978-0-7643-4488-6. $29.99

Copyright © 2014 by Schiffer Publishing, Ltd.

Library of Congress Control Number: 2014940802

Type set in Futura Std/Minion Pro

ISBN: 978-0-7643-4434-3
Printed in United States of America

Published by Schiffer Publishing, Ltd.
4880 Lower Valley Road
Atglen, PA 19310
Phone: (610) 593-1777; Fax: (610) 593-2002
E-mail: Info@schifferbooks.com

For our complete selection of fine books on this and related subjects, please visit our website at www.schifferbooks.com. You may also write for a free catalog.

This book may be purchased from the publisher.
Please try your bookstore first.

We are always looking for people to write books on new and related subjects. If you have an idea for a book, please contact us at proposals@schifferbooks.com.

Schiffer Publishing's titles are available at special discounts for bulk purchases for sales promotions or premiums. Special editions, including personalized covers, corporate imprints, and excerpts can be created in large quantities for special needs. For more information, contact the publisher.

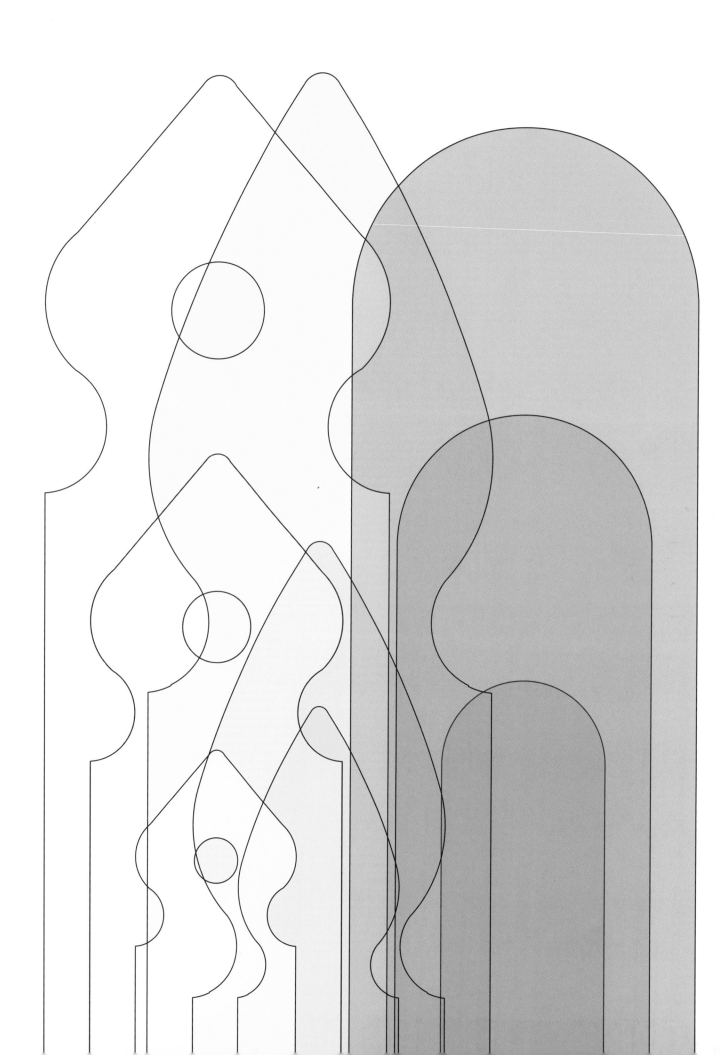